Living With The Bunnies

Fiona Barrett

iUniverse, Inc.
New York Bloomington

Living With The Bunnies

iUniverse books may be ordered through booksellers or by contacting:

iUniverse
1663 Liberty Drive
Bloomington, IN 47403
www.iuniverse.com
1-800-Authors (1-800-288-4677)

ISBN: 978-1-4401-1203-4 (sc)
ISBN: 978-1-4401-1204-1 (ebook)

Printed in the United States of America

iUniverse rev. date: 1/30/2009

Dedication

To Jenn and Sista Rose. For making it all worthwhile, for your endless hospitality and for all the laughs. Friends for life are not made everyday, I am lucky to have made two in you. Thank you.

Forward

In March 2004, on Mothers Day infact, myself, Fiona (otherwise known as Princess Shrek), hubby Nigel (strong, silent type), and our four kids, Abbie aged 9, twins Sam and Ben aged 7, baby Leo aged eleven months and the family dog, Rafferty, set off from deepest Hertfordshire for a life in sunny California, USA. Marin County to be exact, that's just over the Golden Gate Bridge and home to the likes of Sean Penn, Santana, Huey Lewis and the Botox bunnies. I started to write mass emails on a regular basis to friends and family telling of our adventures and about what it was really like to live in the State where 'movies' are made and stars are born and how the inhabitants cannot tell movies from reality and put said stars in positions of immense power like Governor of State, but lets not get me started on that one until later!

We lived with the bunnies for three and a half years before returning to Ole Blighty in 2007 where we submerged ourselves back into reality again and where a cup of tea solves most problems and complete strangers at bus stops are happy to discuss their hemorrhoids!

Ohh, it's good to be back. I do hope you enjoy the newsletters, according to hubby we will never be allowed back into the States as I will have a Fatwa on my head like Salman Rushdie!

Table of Contents

LIVING WITH THE BUNNIES
A BRITISH FAMILYS' EXILE TO MARIN COUNTY.

Sarah Palin got Pit bulls with lipstick, I got bunnies with botox!

Contents

March 23rd, 2004

WE'RE HERE!

Well, we have finally arrived at our new abode in California! We had a dead posh flight over, I even had a manicure on board. The kids loved flying 1st class, it was movie after movie. Leo charmed the air stewardesses and was generally a sweetheart for the whole 9 ½ hour flight. It was fab that he could actually sleep in a proper bed and the cabin crew were great. I am a 'Virgin' lover, whoo hoo! The kids of course did not sleep a wink for the entire flight and as a result fell asleep the minute we got into the car at this end to bring us to our new 'home' and missed their first ever view of the Golden Gate Bridge!

It was deffo a weird feeling landing in an unfamiliar country to a place totally alien to you and knowing that this was 'home' for the foreseeable future. I must confess to feeling quite tearful, which only got worse once we arrived at the apartment complex.

We are living at a place called Larkspur Landing, a fifteen minute drive north of the Golden Gate Bridge. It's a complex of new apartments built on a hill overlooking the ferry terminal which takes you into San Francisco. Below the apartments there is shopping area with some restaurants, hairdressers and a yoga studio but nowhere to buy a pint of bloody milk!

The actual complex is nice with a kids play area and a pool and even has a gym which is all free to residents, might get to look like Spammy Pammy yet!

The relocation guy who found us the place is so obviously young and single that he really didn't think too hard about somewhere appropriate to place a family of 6 with a baby and a dog! We are on the first floor, no lift and the car park is in a different building! I have matching bruises on each leg from lugging the pram up and down the steps as well as having the dilemma of doing the weekly shop and deciding which is worse. Leaving a baby in a car whilst making several trips, with shopping bags, into the apartment or leaving a baby alone in the apartment whilst I fetch the shopping!

Last night I counted I climb 27 steps to the apartment, 89 steps to the car and a further 98 steps to put my bin bags out for collection.

We have GOT to move.

The actual apartment is nice enough but everything is cream or white, I am permanently walking behind Leo with a bottle of ' carpet cleaner' as he barfs over the shagpile!

It was great when Raffy arrived, though there's no garden so it's a major task to let him out for a tinkle. At night I pull a jumper over my pajamas and walk around the complex having a good gawp through the windows! Tibetan terriers are very popular here, there are at least 3 living in this complex!

Nige gets the ferry each morning, he says it's a lovely 25 minute trip across the Bay and then a short walk up to his office. He even has his own office with a nice view of the city, my view from the apartment is that of wheelie bins from the hotel behind us..ho hum.

Now the kids are over the jet lag it's time to find them a school. Yippee, I can smell freedom. Actually we'll all kill each other if we stay cooped up in this flat much longer!

Ta Ra. for now.

Larkspur Landing Apartments

April 15th, 2004

FROM THE BIRD ON THE BAY

Not a great time since my last newsletter! We have discovered we live next door to 'Heda', from Single White Female! She has taken it upon herself to educate me of every petty rule laid down for residents of this 'exclusive' complex. Now, these apartments are made of clapboard and the passage ways are all wooden planks. She has informed me that kids are not allowed to make a noise outside of their apartment before 8am and that my kids, therefore, must remove their shoes when passing her apartment which we need to do every time we leave our own. This is a bit difficult seeing as we leave at 7:45am to do the school run.

Yesterday I put a full bin bag outside my apartment whilst I got showered and dressed so that Raffy didn't get to it as the apartment is open plan there is nowhere to shut him in.

Tap, tap goes the front door. Heda then gives me a lecture on the different types of diseases that flies carry here in California and can I please not leave a 'trash bag' outside again.

The next run in we had was at the pool. The kids and I were the only ones there so we had a fun game of volley ball in the water. After a while 'Speedo Man' comes in and lies on a lounger next to the pool with his newspaper. He's about 60 years of age with dyed red hair and obscene tiny black Speedo swimming trunks. His chest hair alone could be used for a commercial for a carpet company. Erlack!!

Within 10 minutes he stands up and shouts,

"Hey lady, cantcha read? It says no goddamn f**king ball games in the pool." We were all stunned into silence, well, I was for about 10 seconds! I asked him not to use language like that in front of myself and the children and that there was really no need to be quite so rude and aggressive. Well, he just went on and on. The kids got out and then asked me what we should do about the ball that was still in the pool. I whispered to them that on the count of three to cannonball into the water.

It was fantastic! It was like a tidal wave hit him, serves him right!

So, I don't think much of the locals so far.

Last week the kids all started at school. They are in two different schools in a place called San Rafael. I cried when I dropped them all off. Poor Abbie is in a school on her own which is very ethnically mixed and she is in the minority group. The drive there was terrifying and I had a meltdown in case I couldn't find my way back to pick them up. I am still struggling with the driving, especially if I am turning left! I have also learned that you can turn right on a red traffic light if the road is clear! Apparently if you are staying longer than a year then you have to pass your test here. Oh poo! As if that is not bad enough if you move from one State to another you have to repeat the driving test for that State!

Most scary is the fact that I have not seen ONE driving instructor….!

There is no such thing as a roundabout and there are STOP signs on all residential cross roads instead of traffic lights. It's all very confusing! There does not appear to be any law on what condition your car is in and there are some right old bangers on the roads! I am driving a 'Sherman Tank' otherwise known as a Dodge Caravan. The name may change on the outside but it's just another 'Barrett Bus' to me!

The weather is really lovely; it's daily in the 80's but is not humid at all. When Leo naps I sun my buns on the balcony with some very carefully placed towels over the railings, if one of them slipped then Heda really would have something to complain about!!

So, life is sort of getting into a routine. I do feel very devoid of adult company, well nice and not abusive adult company anyway! I know things are bad as last night I cut Nigels' dinner up for him and started making train noises with the fork. Job for the week, must find alternative brain stimulation.

Ta Ra for now.

May 27th, 2004

GREETINGS Y'ALL

Have now found a treatment for mushy brain! I have enrolled myself on a degree course in Criminal Justice. Not entirely sure what use it will be if I ever need to use it to get a job outside of the U.S. but at least it will keep the grey matter from shriveling to the size of a walnut. Felt quite excited, I can have a conversation with other people that's not about the digestive system of babies or dry dog food verses wet. Fantabulous!

Nige got himself a little 'runaround' last weekend. A silver, top of the range Audi Convertible little 'runaround' and Oh, it's only got two seats. So, a truly practical vehicle for a family of six then! How come I only ever get a bus and he only ever gets the penile extension?!

Now I'll get off the soapbox. Grr

Seeing as in a fortnight the kids break up for the summer holidays, 10 weeks of sheer purgatory, we have decided to rent a Winnibago and go traveling! We are planning on following Route 1 which hugs the coast, all the way down to San Diego, staying at various Camp America sites along the way. Abbie and I are desperate to stop off in L.A. to see the sights and the boys just want to do the Disney parks. I am busy planning our route and booking camp sites. Am really excited!

I have managed not to upset any locals, they just don't seem very chatty and they do seem rude. Often if I pass someone when I'm out with the dog I meet other people and I make a greeting of some kind. Nine times out of ten they will not respond at all and just pretend not to have heard me! As for their driving manners! They will not let you cut into a queue for love nor money. I have also realized that if you flash your lights to let someone pass they have no idea what you mean. They rely on hand signals or yelling or the preferred method of driving etiquette is to lean on the horn for a minimum of 15 seconds!

Abbies' school recently held an 'International' day where there were stands selling food and displaying goods for the various countries/cultures at the school. The majority of the kids at her school are Hispanic and so Spanish is their first language. We won some Mother & Daughter belly dancing lessons…not a pretty thought after four kids. Yuck!

We have finally found a house to move into in July! Yippee and goodbye Heda and Speedo Man. It is in a place called Kent Woodlands and is high up on a mountain called Mount. Tamalpais. It was built in the 1960's, (the house, not the mountain.), and really has not had much done to it since then, but, it is huge and has great views over the East Bay looking towards Berkeley. Best of all it has a pool and it's a drive to the nearest neighbors. Yay!

It will also mean the kids moving school as, apparently, if you move areas then your kids have to change schools too.

So, some change afoot. Till next time

Adios Amigos

June 29th, 2004

NICE TO SEE YOU, TO SEE YOU NICE

Well it was lovely to see many of you earlier this month when we came home for Siobains' wedding! I was rather pleased that I did not resemble an aubergine too much after losing 10lbs since being in the States. It was a lovely day and the weather perfect.

It was really quite hard to return back here after being back home with everyone. It has made me miss friends and family even more. I think that because I knew we would be going home to the U.K. again after only being here for nine weeks it gave me something to look forward to. Now I know that I won't see home or any family until Christmas and it seems a very long way away. Whilst I am always busy here, I really do miss the English sense of humour and having a real belly laugh. You know when you laugh so hard that your tea comes out your nose! Must stop maudlin, we move into the new house in two weeks and I have not even started to pack yet!

Will write again once we are in residence. Can't believe I am moving for the second time in a year, at least this time it's a mile up the road and not six thousand across water!

Ciao!

July 18th, 2004

THE NEW ABODE

We are finally in our new abode and it feels great! There was not a huge amount for us to do as we only really had clothes in the apartment and Leos' cot and highchair. It feels so good to have all our things out of storage and around us again. It makes us feel a lot more at home. Ten weeks it took for all our things to arrive from England, and we filled a forty-foot container!

The house is fabulous and just so big! The downstairs is open plan with windows all across the front to take in the amazing views. There is a basement that we have made into a play room that has its own deck off it. There is no garden as such, although the house sits on an acre of land (American acres are smaller than ours) it sits on top of a hill. The majority of the gardens are unusable but there is a huge deck built all around it. The drive is scary, its 180 feet long and spirals with a huge drop on one side! That should be fun in the dark as there are no street lights!

There is plenty of wild life around too. There are hundreds of little lizards, running everywhere, I keep the doors shut in case they come in! The boys keep trying to catch them and the dog is scared of them! No snakes yet but I have seen plenty of deer.

Thankfully, all the houses here have screens on the windows to prevent anything crawling in! In the garage we found a cupboard full of wine! Some of it looked quite old, I have resisted opening any in case the landlady knows it is there!

She seems really nice, she is a Sculptress, though hopefully nothing like the one played by Dawn French! The owners have never lived in this house but want to rent it out for a few years before doing a 'remodel' and moving in themselves. It's a bloody big house for two people, 4,000 sq. feet and they are in their 60's.

We have had a couple of fun days out recently. Last week we went to the infamous Alcatraz! The island sits a mile off land in the San Francisco bay. We got a little boat over to it; there is a lighthouse at one end of the island that still flashes to warn ships entering the bay under the Golden Gate Bridge. Despite it being a beautiful day it was really cold on the island, there was a strong cold wind blowing.

It all looks overgrown now and the seagulls seem to be gradually taking over the island. It was really eerie walking around and seeing where the guards lived and their gardens and the parade ground.

We did an audio tour; some of the previous inmates are now the tour guides and tell some amazing stories! To see all the cells, some still kitted out as they would have been in its heyday and hearing the story of the Great Escape and looking at the bullet holes in the roof where the army blasted its way in was totally fascinating. Abbie bought a book called Al Capone does my shirts written by one of the Guards children and Nige and I bought a book as thick as the bible about the history of the island. I also saw a really cute escapee babygrow in black and white but Nige refused to let me buy it. Might wait till he's in Japan…

We have also had a trip to Angel Island which is an island off Tiburon. It was California's equivalent to Staten Island and was therefore the first point of entry for immigrants arriving in San Francisco. Now it is mainly a nature reserve. There is a trolley bus that you can take around the island with an audio tour to learn of its history as an immigration station. It only takes five minutes to get to from Tiburon and has a very pretty harbour with a café and a strip of sandy beach. We spent our time admiring all the beautiful boats moored up and chasing after Leo who kept shuffling on his bum towards the sea! He keeps the floors at home buffed up nice and shiny!

It was very easy to imagine we were on the med, sat on the beach overlooking the harbour and watching the gulls soaring overhead. We could also see seal lions sunning on the rocky outcrops and some pelicans bobbing on the waves. It was ever so peaceful.

So, another week over.

That's my news, what's yours?

Hillbilly House

Pool at Hillbilly house.

View from Hillbilly House looking over the East Bay towards Berkley.

August 8th, 2004

THE PIKEYS' RETURN TO WALTON MOUNTAIN

As they say over here, we had an awesome time!

We might actually smell a little bit and some of us may not have 'changed our shoes', (had a number two!) but we had a great adventure!

Here is a summary of our Camp America stops.

Santa Cruz-fabulous campsite. Horse corral, Go Karts and a pool. Woke up to cold grey skies and thought I was in Cornwall. Bought a nasty jumper at a campsite shop. The town itself was exactly how I imagine the Midwest to be. One road with a solitary petrol station, a seedy café, a hardware store and . . . six antique shops??

Santa Margarita-weather really hot and have ditched the nasty jumper!

This place is in the middle of nowhere with dry dirt roads and hard standing for the Winnebago. It did have a swimming pool though. We had campfire dinners at night by candle light.

We then had a scenic drive along Route one which is known as the Big Sur, and follows the sea all along to Los Angeles.

Los Angeles-this campsite was really a car park in the fairgrounds of the city. Each city has an area called The Fairgrounds and is used to host all large outdoor events like concerts and circuses.

We awoke at 6am to the roar of Harley Davidsons' screeching around a track!

It was sooo worth it though, we spent one day at Universal studios, one day at Disneyland (Nige and I want to get jobs there, I reckon I'd be good as one of the dwarves) and the best day in Hollywood!

Abbie and I were beside ourselves with excitement for this day. We arranged to go on a bus tour around the Stars Homes, Beverley

Hills and Hollywood itself. When the bus arrived, we were the only people who had booked and so we had the tour guide to ourselves!

It was nothing at all like I had imagined it, we saw some filming in the oldest part of L.A and were able to get out and watch. It was for a television series for a Spanish viewing channel so we didn't understand a word!

Hollywood Boulevard is really quite rundown and shabby. We did, however do the walk of Fame following the stars hand prints and had a peek in the Kodak theatre where the Academy Awards are held. We also stood outside the Chinese theatre where there were lots of characters dressed up for you to pose with. We tried to get Bugs Bunny to hold Leo for a photo but he burst into tears! That was Leo, not Bugs bunny!

We drove down Sunset Boulevard (no sign of Hugh or Divine!), past The Viper club owned by Johnny Depp and where River Phoenix collapsed and died.

A mile or so along and we reached Beverley Hills. Huge, colossal houses, Aaron Spellings' place has 120 rooms, saw Barbara Streisands' house, The Playboy Mansion, Dr. Phils', (he parks his car on the street outside) and best of all I sat outside BRAD PITTS house!!! Aghhh!!

I was probably on his security camera as there were loads of them in the bushes around the house. He's probably trying to track me down as I type...

Did we actually see anyone famous I hear you ask? Well, yes we saw Sharon Osborne out walking the dogs. I did shout coo ee and she did wave back!

Next, we drove down Rodeo Drive, the locals pronounce it Row Day O! Nige was panicking incase the driver stopped to let us out in the shops! $$$$$$$$$$$

Then it was off to

SanDiego - almost on the Mexican border, so getting very hot now. Nice beach town. Spent a day at the Wild life park, which is in the desert. Just like doing a safari, well worth a visit and stunning scenery. The staff working at these places are just so nice and accommodating!

Lake Isabella - drove in the night to get here following a river. Passed a couple getting down and dirty in a flatbed truck! Being high up in the Winnie I got quite an eye full! A truly horrid campsite. Woke up the next morning to people peering through the windows! We were in the only vehicle with wheels! When I went to pay, the woman just looked blankly at my Visa card! Real Redneck country!

Yosemite - most beautiful place I have ever been. Majestic mountains, trees called Sequoias, some of them date back to the times of Cleopatra. Some are so tall and thick you can walk through the trunks. Spectacular waterfalls, we paddled in the rivers. Full of deer but thankfully, no Grizzly bears since 1924. The park was originally home to the Miwok Indians, a small village remains where the Indian descendents return for certain ceremonies and traditions.

The actual campsite was basic but lovely. We sat under these giant trees and had a BBQ at night. We were awoken at 4:15 am by what I thought was a bear rocking the Winnebago!

There are warnings throughout the park warning you not to leave any food in tents or cars as the Black Bears will be in to get it as they can smell food from a mile away. After a few seconds we realized it was an Earthquake! Very scary when you are 5,000 feet above sea level and directly under 100 ft tall trees! Where exactly do you go? It only lasted a minute and we were all fine. How exciting!

Upon leaving the Park the following day we saw some fires in the distance. We were going down a narrow track and could see the helicopters dropping water onto the fires. Before we realized it, we were trapped in the road which was too narrow to turn around on and too difficult to reverse back. In true British style I put the kettle and Nige got the Camcorder out whilst we waited to be rescued! In due course a police escort arrived and we were saved!

Stockton - arrived at the campsite at 1 am and was awoken every 15 minutes there after. We were parked next to the railway line!

So, now we are back to reality, school starts soon which means me being the soccer mum. Abbie has training twice a week, matches on Saturdays, as do the boys but their training is on different days! I do manage to get Wednesdays off!

Phew.

Adios for now!

Kids next to Winniebago

August 19th, 2004

HILLBILLY NEWS

Phew we've had a hot one!

The weather got hotter and hotter as the week progressed and I became busier and busier! I have done the new school meetings at both Abbies' and the boys' school which went really well. The only real anxiety is that not only are the boys starting yet another new school but they will be separated for the first time ever. It is apparently the school policy and they are not flexible on it. I did think this was a bit rough on the boys, new country, new school and now this. Time will tell . . .

They all start tomorrow so Nige is going in with Abbie and I will take the boys.

Both schools seem very well equipped and have fabulous computer labs and a really good library which are open at break or 'recess' too. Lots of clubs are run at lunch times too

i.e., astronomy, film, bands

Abbies' school has two full time councilors for the kids, twice a month school finishes early so that teachers and councilors can discuss any problems regarding individuals. At least by doing this you will not get kids 'slipping' through the net and not getting the help and support they need.

All class sizes are 'capped' at twenty which is great. There are different numbers of kids per year as they have to provide more classrooms and teachers if the school has a particularly big intake in a year. Here, the local authority is obliged to offer a child a place at the nearest school but, if you move out of the catchment area then the child has to be removed! We have had to provide proof of an address with our rent agreement as well as copies of utility bills!

Parents are expected to be very involved with the schools on a voluntary basis and can be expected to assist with dinner lady duties, playground supervision and even manning the phones in the office! Each family is asked to contribute $25 towards the PTA but then that's it.

Last Wednesday we had an informal night in the playground to meet the teachers and other parents, the school laid on a Buffet and drinks so it was all very relaxed.

What is strange is that there is no school cafeteria so all the kids eat at tables outside. I wonder what happens in the winter?

The other parents seemed nice enough, they were all dead glamorous, I reckon I was the only one who had never had botox, not a wrinkle to be had amongst the lot of them!

What do you suppose they'll make of me when I turn up at the school gates in my wellies and yellow mac?

Next Friday we have been invited to someone's house (no idea who they are!) for hors d'oeuvres and canapés! Who the feck wants to eat horses' hooves in a friggin' tent? What's wrong with cheese and pineapple on a stick? Still, nice of them to ask and Nige thinks we should go as all the parents from Sam and Bens year will be there . . . have to admit it sounds the sort of situation that makes me cringe and I am bound to say the wrong thing!

I am now officially a soccer mum and have met a lot of really nice mums at training sessions which are always good fun. Many of the kids go to the same school as Sam and Ben so there should be some familiar faces for them when they go tomorrow.

These Marin folk do take everything very seriously, once all the soccer teams have decided on a team name they then have a Banner Party. Am not quite sure how it happened but somehow I found myself with the job of making the banner for Sam and Bens team . . .

On Saturday we were all up at 7 am as there was a grand parade for all the teams to show off their team banners and have team photos taken. There was also an award for the best banner. Imagine my horror when I saw all the other banners. I kid you not they were A level works of art! They were all huge, many of them hand sewn and quilted with brass poles supporting them on either side. My effort was a picture of the Forever Friends Bears wearing the team colours, drawn on a bit of white card supported with an old garden cane! We didn't win. .

By 8am it was 80 degrees and by the afternoon when twenty-five teams were playing matches it was 97 degrees! It was all so well organized, there were tents for each team, the kids were subbed often and all sprayed with cold water when they came off the pitch. Apparently the parents of each team take it in turn to provide drinks and snacks for the whole team for each game. The atmosphere was really good, the matches went on until 4:30 pm, Abbie was made Captain and lots of comments were made about how pleased everyone was to have some English kids playing as they are considered much better at soccer than the Americans, so that was nice.

I did, embarrassingly, get asked to Be Quiet by the Ref! Apparently parents are not encouraged to shout and cheer from the sidelines, not like Rugby then!

Actually, the Ref did come over at the end of the game laughing and said that all he could hear on the pitch was my gob!

At the end of the day it was really lovely to come home, don the cozzie and jump in the pool! Great day!

To-day we went to a local park for a picnic and watched a baseball game and then we went off to another park for a party that was organized to get all the people that live on the Mountain together to get to meet their neigbours. It was really lovely, there was a treasure hunt for the kids and lovely food and wine set out for the adults. When we arrived at this park, it is called a Garden Centre but doesn't sell plants but it does have an antique shop and also has an outdoor amphitheatre. Sean Penn lives next door!

There was a table with loads of information about the area and cards from people advertising babysitters and dog walkers and leaflets on local Halloween parades and all sorts of useful info. Everyone seemed really friendly, it was nice to see some neighbours as all the houses are set very far back and far apart so you never know who lives next door! Again there were kids there that go to the same school as ours will go to. I met a great Irish girl who writes crime novels set in Ireland so we got on really well!

So, a really busy week and a really nice week-end. I am all prepared for tomorrow but feel anxious for all of them but I am definitely looking forward to some time on my tod too! I worked out the kids have only been in school for three weeks since we arrived in the U.S. because of us returning home for three weeks!

Will let you know how it all goes.

Ta Ra. for now!

September 13th, 2004

MOUNT TAM NEWS WEEKLY

A nice week had by all, that is except for one minor hiccough. My darling hubby bought a chair from Macys' Department store. It is a very nice chair. However, it does not match anything whatsoever in our living room! We have a Royal blue couch and a blue and yellow couch. The chair he bought is an orange/red and gold.

Why Oh why can't he be like every other man I know and show no interest whatsoever in decor? I swear if I mentioned that I needed to buy a new set of teaspoons he would just love to come and choose some with me!

Anyway, I decided to solve the problem by dying the covers of the blue couch red and by putting a red throw over the blue and yellow couch. Just ask yourselves what colour do you get if you mix Red and Blue? To make matters even worse I had bought some pretty voile curtains to replace the truly hideous Hessian ones in the living room. So, I took down the old curtains which was a huge effort as they are more than 7 feet high and the room is 30 feet long and, they were on a pulley system.

Alas, the new curtains didn't fit and I couldn't get the old ones back up! By the time Nige returned home from work we had a purple couch, no curtains and I had drowned my sorrow in a bottle of Rioja and was giggling manically on the floor, only for him to announce he had invited some work colleagues for dinner the following night!

So, by 7:15 am the following morning I had cooked two huge lasagnas and legged it to the shops and bought slip covers for both couches (in red) and new curtains!

On Monday it was my turn to host the botox mother and toddlers group and only one turned up! I have since sent them all a sarcastic email and have ungraciously withdrawn from the group. I must confess to buying a book that one of them wrote though!

I am now slightly mortified as I have met up with a couple of mums from school who all have boys the same age as Leo. It was our first get together this week and we met up at one of their houses. The host was a bloody neat freak and even gave me a silver peeler to peel grapes for the babies!! She is now known in our house as Immaculate Monica. She even had some Child Proof specialist come into her house and nail everything to the floor or wall!

We were sitting talking about our homes (as you do at these meetings?!) and I was saying our home was great because the landlords are really relaxed about the décor / furnishings as they are going to gut the house entirely once we have left. Well, Immaculate Monica gave me a lecture about how relaxed I was about housework and that I was therefore setting a bad example and would be teaching my kids bad habits! Just imagine her face if she had been here with the couch and curtain saga! It's my turn to host the next meeting. Maybe if I don't eat, sleep or use the bathroom my house could look like hers! Or, I could just say, "Sod it, take me as you find me."

We have done a lot of hiking and exploring recently. After Nigels' dinner guests left, we decided to walk to the top of the mountain on which we live.. Maybe Nige was thinking of shoving me off after the couch fiasco.

The walk was beautiful; from our house the view stretches 40 miles across the bay. The hills are all dotted with remote homes painted in pastels and terra cottas and look like a picture of somewhere on the Med. From behind us, going up the mountain it was like some Norwegian forest with towering conifers creating a stunning skyline. At the very top there is a Lookout used and manned by the Fire Brigade to watch for the ever feared fires that hit this area each year at about this time. It was a lovely walk but we still have to be wary and walk with a large stick and rocks in our pockets in case of a chance encounter with a mountain lion or coyote. It does make me anxious taking Raffy Roo on these hikes as he would make a lovely dinner!

We have also found a lovely State Park, of which California has more of than any other State, in a place called Fairfax. This is a town 15 minutes west of us here in Kentfield and is where the Hippie movement first started. It's pretty amazing the difference in the people over such a short distance. In Fairfax everyone is much more relaxed and informal and friendly. There is a real sense of community and there are lots of pubs with live bands and fun little restaurants and wonderful shops and places to have Reiki and massages. Whereas Kentfield is all about Lawyers and botox clinics and people wearing lots of Lycra!

The park itself does cost $5 to enter but is like an African Game Reserve with lots of wildlife and huge reservoirs all surrounded by rolling hills in various shades of gold and green. We walked around a lake called Lake Laguinitas where we could see turtles swimming and red-tailed Kites soaring majestically overhead. Obviously all this peace and tranquility was totally blown away by our four screeching and running full tilt though the woods shouting Swallows and Amazons forever, like a scene from a Victoria Wood sketch!

Despite this it was very lovely and wore the buggers out which is always a good thing!

The boys have a big presentation to do at school tomorrow and have been rehearsing to Nige and I. I am horrified to hear an American twang creeping in already!

My Mother will have a fit!

Nigel and Raffy at Lake Laguinitas

October 17th, 2004

WET STUFF!

There's wet stuff falling from the sky, and lots of it! Am I in Cornwall? We seem to have gone from rampant fires and searing heat to cold and damp and drizzle, all within a week.

Ahhh, but it feels like home…

It has been a quiet week for us, we did not get evacuated but the fires did burn for six days. Terribly sad, think of all that wasted venison . .

This week I decided to brighten up the garden and plant some cheap and cheerful tubs around the deck. Buying plants here is so much cheaper, it was quite strange to be in a garden centre in October and buying up plants that we only plant out in the Spring in the U.K!

The shops are full of Halloween goods as it is such a big thing here. We have seen lots of houses with elaborate decorations, apparently many homes are open to go in and look around on the night itself. I must confess to buying into a bit, the kids and I decorated the front of our house with an enormous spider web with suspended insects within it. I don't know why we bothered really, no-one in their right mind is going to heave themselves up our drive on the off chance there are a couple of mint imperials in a bowl on the doorstep!

The kids are really tired now, I can tell they are ready for a break but they won't get one until November when the schools have three days off for Thanks Giving. What's all that about anyway? Answers on a postcard please.

If any of your cherubs moan to you about homework tell them to spare a thought for our lot. They each have 45 minutes a night of the usual Maths and English, on top of which they have to prepare a written report on a Current Event in the local or National newspapers and practice presenting it to the whole class. They also have to use their own time to prepare any projects, at the moment the boys are each writing a project on the history of a local town. They are expected to visit the town and take photos too. By the end of the month both boys are expected to read an entire book and write up a critique about it. All together they average three hours a night!

Thankfully they have Soccer at week-ends for some chill out time. There are just two more weeks left of the season. They all played in matches yesterday. I love to watch them play despite still having zero understanding of the Offside Rule. I have asked for the book A Dummies Guide To Football for a Christmas present!

In February the three of them have been asked to 'tryout' for a 'select' soccer team to play for the County. It sounds great but it is a huge commitment as we would have to travel all over California, staying in Hotels and training three times a week as well as matches on both days at the week-end.

What would I do when Nige is away?

Also, imagine what I would do if they didn't all make it through and I had to drag the one that didn't make it to watch the one that did! Speaking of Thanks Giving, we have decided to bugger off for a long week-end to a place called Mendicino. It is a little artist type town on the coast three hours north of here. It would seem to be California's equivalent of Brighton. It is an old Gold Rush town and apparently you can still pan for gold up there in them darn rivers. Yee Haw Cowboy!

Just a bit random but here are some facts about California

1) California is the 7th biggest economy in the world
2) Its population is higher than that of the whole of Canada
3) It is five times bigger than the entire British Isles!

As for television, all that can be seen at the moment are the Bush V. Kerry debates. Even our kids can all can point on a map which States are Republican and which are Democrat and, they have mini debates as part of the school curriculum. I actually think this is really good, I don't remember learning anything at all about politics when I was at school. California is considered to be very anti-Bush and he does not bother campaigning for votes here. Just about every car you see has a Vote for Kerry sticker on the bumper. I have never seen one for Bush. The Californians are a might deluded though aren't they? I mean they really cannot separate fantasy from reality.

After all, they voted in actor Ronald Reagan for President, Clint Eastwood for Mayor of Carmel and now they have put the bloody Terminator as governor of the whole State!

At the moment he is on TV in some commercial. In it he is standing in a Supermarket holding up an Artichoke and saying, in a thick Austrian accent "Be Californian, buy Californian".

I keep waiting for him to add

"I'll be back".

The Yanks just love it!

I have been quite proud of myself this week, I have been writing letters in Spanish! The reason being that Nige suggested we may be in need of a cleaner after Ben came running downstairs shouting that we had been burgled. This would not have come as a complete surprise considering the number of times I have either left the front door wide open or left the keys in the outside lock!

As it happens, when I went upstairs to investigate I realized that it was merely somewhat untidy, well, a complete mess actually. Therefore, I have now found a nice girl to come and clean for us. The downside is she does not speak a word of English as she is from Sal Salvador in South America, and I , alas, do not know any Spanish.

She did smile and nod a lot though on her first day and I had assumed she had understood my pathetic attempts at communicating. Evidently she did not as when I left I told her she could go at 2pm. Upon returning home at 4:30pm she was still here!

I have now bought a Teach Yourself Spanish book and somehow, between us we communicate and have a jolly good laugh too! I try to write in Spanish what I want her to do, I am quite sure she drives home pissing herself laughing!

Anyway, that's me done. I hope you all enjoy Halloween. I remember taking our kids trick or treating in Potten End when they were very small. Seeing lights on in the Vicarage, we went up to his door. We could see him sitting in the living room. The kids rang the bell and the miserable sod stood up and pulled the curtains closed in front of them and ignored the doorbell! I recall telling all the teenagers we met out that night that the vicar was giving a pound to everyone that knocked on his door!

Do give him a knock from us!

November 29th, 2004

THANKS GIVING GREETINGS TO Y'ALL

Well, we have returned to Walton Mountain following our latest adventure. We had a scenic drive up the coast to Mendicino, but, I must say, I did miss the good old British Pee and Tea stops along our route, especially when one is traveling with little people!

Instead of Moto service stations we ended up stopping in Hicksville and taking our chances! We passed through places with names like Boonsville where they have their own language, apparently when you walk into a shop the locals are really rude and swap lingo. I said we have the same problem in Britain, little place called North Wales…

Mendocino was very pretty, all pastel coloured clapboard houses nestled along the cliffs, much smaller than I had anticipated. Not a family town by all accounts, it was populated almost entirely by 'luvvies', about 60 years of age and wearing tie dye and dreads locks! We went to a local Art festival but it was all too Arty Farty for me and I got a fit of the giggles! We stayed in a place called Fort Bragg which used to be a Logging town, these places I find really weird as they have no town centre as such, it's just a strip of shops along a main road. Our hotel was right on the beach, which the kids just loved as the patio doors opened directly onto the sand. On the first day they found an enormous crab that we had to protect from the seagulls until the tide came in to rescue it! Ben refused to leave until he was sure it was quite safe. Another local beach we visited was called Glass Beach; years ago there was a nearby glass factory which dumped directly into the sea. As a result the whole beach is covered in tiny multi coloured pieces of glass worn smooth by the tides. We collected lots to make a mosaic on a rainy day.

It was not rainy but my goodness it was jolly cold!

On one of our days up there we took a steam train along the Noyo Valley called the Skunk Trail. We meandered through giant Redwood trees, some of which are 340 ft high and 55 feet in diameter! The Valley is virtually uninhabited but for bears, lions and deer. At one stage 3,000 people lived there, but, spent so much of their time trying to keep the forest from engulfing their homes they had no time to work, and so they ended up selling their land back to the lumber companies from which they originally bought from.

There are still a few homes which are really very basic and which rely totally on the once a day train for all their needs.

It was quite beautiful to travel through this raw, unspoilt wilderness. A cultural difference that made me smile was what happened each time the train went through a long dark tunnel. The train driver encourages everyone on board to sing at the top of their voice as they went through… and everybody did! Now correct me if I am wrong but that really would not happen at home?!

Another fun place to visit was a working lighthouse where we walked along the bluffs to see some sea lions. It was so dramatic a coastline, really stunning, although you are reminded that you are in Mountain Lion country and to be extra vigilant. I have now become really quite proficient at walking backwards with a couple of rocks in my hand! Nigel always walks ahead, the kids are in the middle whilst I follow up the rear.

So, all in all we had a great time although I must confess that sharing a room with five other people did give me cabin fever, how Ben ever shares a room with Sam is beyond me, he never shuts up, even in his sleep!

It was lovely to spend some time together and we all seemed to have enjoyed it.

It's only when you drive for a while in this country that you truly begin to appreciate just how big it is. We stayed on the same road for hours and hours and all we saw were mountains. Having said that, I would still not like to stay here permanently, although it is beautiful, it would be difficult to live with all the time. It is so vast and, for the most part it is simply so uncultured. These towns can be so very far apart and there really is nothing to do!

One decision I have made is that in my next life, if there is one, I am returning as a female Sperm Whale! According to marine research the mating season is several months long, they have various partners, sometimes a third party helps out and, AND the male Sperm Whale has a 7 foot long Willy !!!!!!!!!

We arrived back to reality last night; Christmas is SO boring here, no Nativity plays, no Carol services, no Christmas Fayres, just no nothing. Utter pants! It is so politically correct, and it makes me furious! Why do people allow this to happen? Surely if we all said NO then the powers that be would give up trying to enforce these ridiculous ideas upon us? Anyway, time for me to get off my Soapbox and practice deep breathing and my mantra. .

I will not conform, I will not conform, traditions are my culture and my right, I will not be told what to say, I will not conform. . . and. . . relax.

Me with the kids at Glass Beach, Fort Bragg.

December 6th, 2004

HAPPY HANUKKAH

Yes, Hanukkah is the reason for the lack of Christmas Festivities, everyone is bloody Jewish! My three now want one of us to convert to Judaism due to the fact that Hanukkah lasts for seven days and you get three presents each night. They only want one of us to convert so that they still get to celebrate Christmas, therefore, December becomes one long month of receiving presents. I think not. .

Whilst there are no Christmas celebrations there are a few houses done up to resemble Blackpool illuminations! The locals seem to go for decorating the outside of their houses and gardens with lots of lights in the trees. One cannot help but feel that Hyacinth Bouquet would have met her match here.

The house at the end of our road has even put an enormous inflatable Snowman outside their fence, it scares the crap out of Leo every time we drive past!

The weather has been lovely and mild so I am back to walking to school a couple of times a week. The kids all had their last tennis session this week so it has been quite calm in our house for a change!

Nigel left for Japan on Saturday so it has just been me and the kids for the week-end. The boys had yet another sleep over on Saturday night, I feel like I'm running a free Bed & Breakfast here at times!

I am on steroids again at the moment! The first time was in Larkspur Landing when I got a skin reaction to the sun and this time I had developed a very red eye that was just not getting better. I referred myself to an eye hospital, when the Dr. checked my eye he said it appeared I had been exposed to some type of chemical that had burnt my eye. It was only once I was home I realized it must have been caused by the eight bottles of dye it took to dye those bloody couch covers!

To make you appreciate the National Health Service, it cost me more than $200 to see the doctor, I had to pay $20 for the prescription and the insurance company paid for the other $80. I also had to phone twelve doctors before I could find one that could see me.

Talking to friends here who have three kids, they pay $750 - $1,000 a month for medical insurance alone. If you are self employed it would mean that the money comes from your own pocket. Add paying 50% tax and it's really quite scary. You would not want to be a pensioner or have chronic health problems and live here.

It is astounding how many young people you see with 3rd world health conditions that we just don't see in England. Young people who have had strokes are left with deformed arms and legs because they cannot afford Physiotherapy. People with severe cataracts that cannot afford the surgery to remove them. With no insurance the hospitals will save your life and stabilize you but offers' nothing else unless you have the funds to pay for it. It's a two-tier health policy here.

On a lighter note, Nigel came home early this week so I took myself off for some retail therapy which meant only having to go into grown up shops! It was deathly quiet and sometimes I was the only person in the shop. Not like England this close to Christmas!

I went into Nordstrom which is a big department store and was looking at the Clarins counter and discussing various beauty tips with the assistant, who was really helpful which was great till I realized this assistance giving me advice on whether to go for the plum or earth eye shadow was a bloomin' tranny!

Anyway, I bought some winter clothes for coming home at Christmas and some . . . plum eyeshadow!

Next week is the Office Christmas party . . . watch this space.

December 14th, 2004

CHAMP HOUSE

After a frantic week of training we were all up at 7am on Saturday for the All-star soccer games. We heard on Monday that Abbie was through as well as the boys so it was all very exciting!

Sam led his team to a 2-1 victory with a superb header into the back of the net. Abbies' team won their match 4-1 so we had three very happy soccer bunnies in the house!

Me? I am hoarse from yelling from the sidelines. Sam and Bens coach is pushing for them to go for these 'Select' tryouts where they travel all over the State. The boys are starting to give us a really hard time about it now.

Abbie went to an end of season party on Friday and received an award for 'most valuable player' which she was thrilled about.

To celebrate all this we took them all for a slap up lunch on Saturday and let them stuff their faces with as much chocolate ice-cream as they could manage!

To-day the boys went to a party in the city, to a movie theatre owned by their friends' parents. It was in Chinatown in a really cute old fashioned cinema. They had a private viewing of The Polar Express and Napoleon Dynamite. They were very impressed that they did not have to pay for their popcorn!

Nigel, Abbie, Leo and I used the opportunity to go off to an Art Festival being held in an old warehouse in the Marina District in San Francisco, looking out over Alcatraz. It has been a beautiful warm and clear week-end so there were lots of people out flying kites and sitting outside cafes drinking lattés.

The exhibition was of Clay and Glass works, we got the tickets from our landlady who is an artist and who was showing some of her work. We bought a glamorous hand blown red bowl and some original glass jewelry for Abbie and I.

There was a kids' corner so Abbie was right in there making a clay dragon with the help of a local artist who boxed it all for her to bring home. He was a really nice guy and, like me, a huge fan of Monty Python so the two of us stood gigging and acting out sketches from our favourite scenes.

"Lovely day for a crucifixion, gets you out in the open air, crucifixion party to the left please."

We picked up the boys after three hours and stayed in Chinatown for the most fantastic Chinese meal, even Leo tucked in! He's into sushi in a big way so he has a very varied palate!

Tomorrow it is my turn to host the Mother and toddler group, must get those toilets shining for Immaculate Monica!

We did have a truly awful experience last week. There is a really nice little town between Kentfield and Fairfax called San Anselmo. It is very similar to an English town as in it has a proper centre to it. I have been to it before and suggested to Nige that we all went there for lunch. We found a really funky shop on the high street that sold anything from vintage clothes to retro furniture. Whilst Abbie and I had a wander around Nigel took the three boys to a model shop. I was standing in the checkout line to pay for some goods when Nige appeared at the open doorway. Leo was crying in the pushchair and Nige had come to ask me if Leo was due for a feed. As it was my turn in the line, I went to hand over the money to pay for my goods. The vile woman behind the till turned to Nigel and said

"For heaven's sake can't you shut that Goddamn baby up, I'm trying to run a business here. Have you no idea how to discipline it?"

I was totally gob smacked (which is a lot for me) and was stood there with the money still in my hand held out to her. Nigel said "Don't you dare give that woman a single penny" and proceeded to argue with her.

I was so upset I ended up walking out the shop in tears and just went straight home! I could not believe how awful she had been about a baby! It wasn't like I had been pushing him around her shop whilst he cried. Some people here are truly hideous.

On a positive note, I have now almost finished my Christmas shopping!

There is really not much hype here at all. There are no Christmas trees or nativity plays at school or christingle services. The cards in the shops all say 'Happy Holidays' as it is not Politically Correct to say Happy Christmas. It is a world gone mad, and there is no atmosphere at all. I suppose that it is because there are so many different religions here that no one person wants to offend another. Why can we not accept everyone has a different culture and embrace all of them and all celebrate our own? I would love to know all about Hanukkah and what people do for Kwanza. I would not expect someone to give up their customs and traditions so as not to offend me! It drives me mad.

I always recall Nige phoning me from Japan and he roaring with laughter about seeing a gigantic model of Santa Claus nailed to a cross on the side of a huge Department Store in Tokyo!

We all take ourselves and some of our beliefs way too seriously!

December 20th, 2004

LAST ONE OF THE YEAR

Had a really fantabulous week-end! It did not start out too well, we hired 'rent a parent' to look after the kids whilst we stayed at a hotel for the Office Christmas Do. Just as she arrived Leo poohed on the lounge carpet and there was a loud crash from upstairs! Abbie had just dropped the fish tank in the sink and smashed it to pieces! Hey ho, regular day in the Barrett household!

We eventually managed to be on our way after leaving endless phone numbers and giving endless hugs and kisses. That was the first time we have ever left them with someone other than family.

The office Christmas party was being held in a hotel called Mankas in a place called Inverness, about an hours drive west of here. All the roads were called things like Dundee drive and Argyle Street. It was like being back in Glasgow!

The main hotel is like an old fashioned hunting lodge. It has a few rooms but the majority of the accommodation is set out in log cabins dotted around the woods. I think that when property comes on the market the hotel buys them up and turns them into guest suites. After checking in, a porter drove us to our cabin, set on stilts in the trees. It was like something out of a Doris Day film with gingham curtains and fur covers and a real log fire. There were no phones or TV's, just a little sitting room with a taffeta couch and velvet chair. The kitchen looked really old but was deffo a designer retro look. The bed was piled high with faux fur skins and the bathroom was simply gorgeous!

After dropping off our luggage and getting changed we dropped off Leo at a cabin provided by the company with four nannies to look after all the children.

The meal itself was lovely, there were seven courses and the wine kept flowing. We were entertained by a jazz band and a choir singing Christmas Carols! It was the first time we had felt anything remotely festive here.

Eventually we left to find our cabin, and it took several staggers around the woods and a great deal of giggling to find it. There was a hot tub on the deck but we were too piddled to organize getting into it!

The cabin might have been very romantic but it was bloody cold. Knowing we were staying at a hotel and normally finding them too hot I had only packed a slip nightie. I had to keep getting up to put logs on the fire, I could put my hand between the window and the sill!

After a sumptuous breakfast and a vat of coffee we arrived back home. The kids had also had a great time and were out playing tennis with the rent a parent!

That night, thanks to our hangovers we all went to a local Italian for dinner. The owner was British and used to be a Chef at the Savoy in London! It is really lovely to have the kids off school and spend some time just hanging out with them; I can't believe it is their first holiday since starting school in August!

So, that's it. We have been here for nine months, I still feel it is an adventure but one which I do want to return home from! The kids are thriving and are so fit and healthy which is wonderful. They all have that permanent sun kissed tan and Leo is white blonde from all the sunshine! We now have a curly red head, two straight light browns and a blonde curly one. Nige says we should have another baby and see if we get one with black hair, but that's just silly! I think we can all agree that I have done my bit for the population!

As for me, I am still off the ciggies and work out three times a week and really enjoy the outdoor lifestyle. However, it is not home, they don't think like we do (on the whole) and I cannot imagine staying here for ever but I am definitely making the most of it whilst I am here.

It has been a fantastic learning curve, we have seen and done so many new things as a family and made some terrific memories that I hope the children will cherish. I think that most of what they have learned here, good and bad, will help shape their personalities and teach them gratitude and tolerance and to appreciate just how fortunate they are to have this opportunity.

And so, I will continue recording my own memories right here for you all.

Wishing you all a very Merry Christmas and a Wonderful New Year.

January 3rd, 2005

HAPPY NEW YEAR

Here is hoping you all had a wonderful Christmas, because we didn't! It all went pear shaped very early on. Sit down and I'll tell you all about it. We arrived in Chester on December 23rd, it was really lovely to see Mum and there were tears all round. The first hint of a problem was about ten minutes after arriving! The two very large boxes containing EVERYONES presents, including a delivery from Santa, which I had posted ($200) at the beginning of December WITH guaranteed delivery … hadn't.

So, on Christmas Eve I ran like a lunatic around Toys R Us and bought two carts full of more presents. We left a letter from Santa explaining that he had taken the best presents to America but had just got the letter saying we were going to be in England for Christmas and so, Simpkin, the Elf, had posted them a few presents to enjoy in England until they got back to California.

Sister Bev arrives on the 23rd but is not feeling too good. By Christmas day she has been vomiting and has diarrhea and a rip-roaring temperature. Thereby the tone is set for the rest of our Christmas holiday! Each day one of the kids came down with the bug until it was Nigel's turn. So, there was me in my Marigolds cleaning up poo and puke 24 hours a day. Santa's presents arrived on December 29th and there was not a soul well enough to give a damn!

On New Years Eve mum looked after the invalids whilst I went to have the Aromatherapy massage she had bought for me for Christmas. That evening Nigel was feeling better and so we went out with eight friends for a Chinese dinner to celebrate the New Year. We had a really fun night, free wine and dancing all night.

Lots of people staying at my mums' house, I got up the next day, minor hangover, not bad at all.

We had one of mums' infamous cooked breakfasts after which we went upstairs to pack. The taxi was picking us up for the airport at 2pm.

About 12pm I suddenly felt very cold and very sick.

Barfed in a bucket for the next two hours whilst sat on the throne!

Traveled to Heathrow with plastic bags, took six hours instead of three. Arrived at the airport hotel only to find the room booking had been totally messed up and instead of being in adjoining rooms, we were in two separate ones.

We arrived back here where it was peeing down with rain, and there have been 11 inches in the last seven days apparently! The car that was supposed to pick us up didn't so we had to get two separate cars to come home. This was after a long flight of being sat next to a baby with an ear infection who squawked the entire way home...

It is now Tuesday, and I have a snotty nose and a sore throat. I either still have the lurgie or I am allergic to the hamster I picked up for Abbie today as we had promised her one for Christmas!

Who knows, and, quite frankly, who cares?

That is all for now, except to say that when I unpacked everything that Nige had had to pack due to my bum being stuck to a loo not one of my presents had made it back here.

And there endeth the tale.

January 10th, 2005

QUACK, QUACK...

Well, it has rained SO much here that even the ruddy ducks have left!

Honestly, it is either feast or famine here. In the summer we had no rain at all for 4 months and awful fires, now we have widespread flooding and mudslides!

Nigel of course feels right at home… Cornwall?

We have finally all got over our jet lag. Leo started the week getting up at 3:30 am and added an hour each day until at last, this morning it was a reasonable 6:30 am. Only another parent of a toddler would EVER think that 6:30 am is a bloody reasonable hour to get up!

I have to say how quickly we have got use to having a toddler in the house again, since returning here he is truly on his feet. Whilst the rest of the world is dealing with Osama Bin Laden we are busy with Leo Bin Loader! He puts just about everything in the bloody bin!

So far this week he has done a fabulous impression of the Andrex puppy whilst I was in the shower. A whole roll of loo paper over the stairs, next I went to answer the phone after which I found him sat in the shower tray tipping all the shampoo and shower gel down the plug hole! I guess this means it is time to put all those locks on the cupboards and never taking my eyes off him!

Last week-end was the start of the Indoor soccer season; will I never get away from balls? There are no practices so it is just one match every Saturday. Nige is the assistant coach for Abbics' team!

So far her hamster has survived but I don't fancy its chances myself. She puts it in a plastic ball and, of course, what does Leo think you do to a ball? I have rescued it once already, it stayed in her room one night, and the next morning I found she had put the cage on the bathroom floor! The next night we put the cage in the Basement, noisy fecker!

Nigel has finally persuaded me to give ski-ing another go, having tried it with disastrous consequences 4 years ago. I have never laughed so hard in all my life and God, did I wish I had done those pelvic floor exercises!

So, we are off to Lake Tahoe, some 3 hours north of here. There has been 12 feet of snow this week. The only thing I know about the place is that Frank Sinatra owned a casino there called CalNev (it is on the border of Nevada) and the likes of Marilyn Monroe used to hang out there. In fact, it was the last place she was seen in public before her death a few days later.

We are staying at a place called Squaw Valley Lodge which is where the Winter Olympics were held in 1950 something. Personally I think it would be much better for me to be the chalet maid and chief beer taster! Thankfully, while we are there we miss going to the school Tombola. Apparently there is a silent Auction. The tickets alone are $125 - $350 each, before you have bid on anything! You have to attend wearing some ridiculous hat and it is a sit down dinner. The sort of thing up for grabs is to go to Michael Scorseses' house (director of the Goodfellas) and watch the film with him while he provides a running commentary for you. I didn't bother offering my hour of Reflexology…

The kids are back at school this week and I must get some studying done myself.

I hope this finds you all sticking to your New Year Resolutions. Mine was to give up wine for 6 months…… my arse!

January 17th, 2005

I HAVE A DREAM

Happy Martin Luther King Day to you all.

The rain has eventually stopped, now we have a drought, we've had the fires, we've had 40 days of rain, what comes next? A swarm of Locusts?

Would not surprise me!

It has been an Abbie kind of week; she is horrified that in P.E. they are doing Line dancing and Square dancing, with boys! She has done nothing but moan about how sore her feet are from being trodden on but I do note that we have been quite liberal with the lip gloss!

We had a letter home a few weeks back informing us that Abbies' year at school was about to have some 'sex education' as part of their studies. After much discussion, Nigel and I decided that I would 'do the talk' before hand and give her some literature so that we knew how much information she had received and just how informed she was.

So, off I went to the local book shop to arm myself with some age appropriate books. I asked the old boy behind the desk to show me where to find literature on 'the birds and the bees' and he sent me off down to the bloody Nature section. The woman on the phone behind him was almost peeing herself laughing at my embarrassment and the old guy looked totally confused when I tried to explain that it wasn't those kinds of bees I was interested in!

After much ado the phone lady led me to the right books. It all rather reminded me of my own mum doing 'the' talk with me after my guinea pig had its 12th litter and we were REALLY struggling to find homes for them. She obviously did an excellent job as I went to school and told just about everyone and mum ended up giving 'the' talk to all my buddies as their parents were too embarrassed!

On Saturday we had been invited by some parents on Abbies' soccer team to their summer cabin on the Russian River. This is an area an hour and a half North East of here in the wine country, near a place called Santa Rosa. We had a really wonderful day, their garden leads directly onto the river and they keep Kayaks to take out for a paddle. They had invited all of their neighbours for a BBQ and we had huge slabs of steak just thrown onto the fire pit. After eating, all the kids chilled out with a movie whilst all the adults sat around the fire laughing and sharing stories. It was a really nice day with some genuine warm people.

On Sunday I took the kids into San Fran as Nige had to leave for Japan. We visited a great museum on the main Dock road called the Musee De Mechaniques which was in a scene in The Princess Diaries 1. It is basically a fruit machine arcade except all the machines date back to the Victorian Era and onwards including a Pac-man from the 1980,s. It is free to enter and all the machines cost 25 cents (12p)!

A little surprise was waiting for us when we got home. It would seem that Herman the Hamster is in fact Hermione and she had duplicated herself many times over! According to the book there could be up to 14 of the noisy little feckers! Needless to say I am the only one who wants to sue the bloody pet shop as the kids are all ecstatic. The blinking receipt said it was a boy!

I had the kids on the phone pronto to all their friends offering free hamsters. I did phone one friend and tried to say that it was an English custom to give pet offspring as gifts to special friends. She said that here in the United States they actually pay people to remove rodents from their homes rather than voluntarily bringing them in. Point taken. The problem is we have to get rid of them all within five weeks as they will become sexually mature and ready to reproduce themselves! God help me!

This week at school we had to prepare an 'Earthquake' kit for the school to keep incase of a major hit! This included a toy, drink, cereal bar and a torch. Whenever you buy or rent a house here, you are, by law, issued with an information pack on how best to prepare your home incase of an Earthquake occurring. This included securing all bookcases and tall objects to the walls and having enough food and water to last the whole family for three weeks. As a result we have now stocked up a huge cupboard in the basement with dried food, blankets, radio, batteries, torches and a small gas stove.

My worst fear is that one happens and I can't get to the kids if they are at school

Speaking of Martin Luther King and dreams. I had a dream about that awful shop owner in San Anselmo, who said dreams can't come true?

Watch this space…

January 24th, 2005

THIS WEEK FROM THE BAY AREA

All is well over on this side of the pond. It has not rained for an entire week so things are looking up! It is, however, rather chilly, and by that I mean I am wearing a jumper and on a really cold day, a coat!

The garden looks positively Spring like, the Camellias are in flower as are the Daffodils. The Geckos must be hibernating as I haven't seen any about for a few weeks now.

I did have a truly horrendous time last week. We came home one day after school and I saw that I had left the side gate open by mistake. Knowing that the deer will eat anything in the garden, I hurried over to close it. As we walked around the back of the house a cat shot across our path. Raffy Roo took off in hot pursuit. The reason the cat was running was there was a full sized deer running in a blind panic behind it! I had obviously, inadvertently, cut off its escape route.

Well, Raffy was so excited, and he didn't know which one to chase. I shoved the kids through the back door and took off after Raffy. The cat had disappeared and so, I thought had the deer. However, Raffy was still very excited and barking at the log pile. When I went to look, the bloody deer had missed jumping the fence and had collapsed between the log pile and the fence. I managed to get the dog in the house. I phoned the Humane Society who told me I needed to confirm the deer was alive as this would affect the outcome of the service they could provide. I went out to check on the deer and the poor thing had died!

I had to plead with the Humane Society to come out that day to remove it as they were willing to leave it lying there until the following Monday! Two hours and $75 later it was gone. We were all quite traumatized. When I told Nigel so was he, he wanted to know why we hadn't just put it in the freezer!

At least our most recent house guest is still fit and well. Last week Leo was sitting at his little table by the window eating his dinner. He kept laughing and saying,

"kangaroo goes boing."

When I eventually went to see what he was laughing about there was a Raccoon jumping up and down from the fence to the deck watching Leo eat! Now I know what it is that keeps pinching the bird food and chucking the bowl over the fence! I have seen a trail of footprints around the pool where he obviously drinks from. Yucky!

I have tried putting a bowl of freshwater out for him but he just paddles in it and tips the water over the deck! He is very funny, he comes each night and sits outside the window tormenting poor Raffy and does not bat an eye when Raffy is barking fit to burst!

Whilst we are on animals, Hermione and babies are doing well. We still don't know how many there are as you are advised not to disturb the nest. Nigel says it looks like a mass of maggots, gross!

At school I have been promoted to Car duty! This basically means I get to stand and open car doors and help kids get out their cars. Due to the fact that there is nowhere to park, as the school is on a main road, parents have to pull in and do a slow drive by to let the kids hop out. The queue can tail right back onto the main road if people are slow. It's a bit like a conveyer belt; four parents stand in a semi-circle and open the doors to speed up getting all the cars through. In the afternoons one person gets the enviable task of having a Bullhorn to holler the kids' names when their respective parents arrive. I can't wait till I get promoted to that roll! Actually, there are many who would say that I don't actually need a Bullhorn…

I have rather mixed feelings about the school. It is definitely very female oriented. There are very few male teachers and they are very 'hot' on some things but seem really lax on others. The teachers all dress informally, food and drinks are allowed in the classroom. Some even bring in pizza for the kids as a reward for good behavior, which is great. However, if they forget a pencil they can get one shoe taken off them for the rest of the day?! They also have a system called a self management card. If a child does something wrong then they receive one of these cards. If they get four in a month then the parents are informed and a plan of action put in place. All this sounds fine but it can be really, really petty. Not long after the boys started, I picked them up from school. Within minutes of getting in the car Ben was in tears, I found out that he had received one of these cards because I had not signed his reading log! I was furious that because of a mistake I had made Ben had been punished! I did march in to see his teacher and said I thought it was a bit over the top. Bearing in mind that we were all new to the school as well as the country and that we were not familiar with this system and that Ben should be cut some slack and each childs' circumstances were different and this should be taken into account. The teacher was decent about it but I felt it was a sure way for Ben to get uptight and upset unnecessarily. He just loves school and was totally mortified at being disciplined this way. Why could she not just explain to him or, even wiser, contact me? On the plus side, the parents are expected to sign these management cards and I will not be signing any more for reasons like this. I am all for supporting the school and in favour of discipline but let's get some things into perspective! Can you imagine what this school would do if you dumped these teachers in an inner city Secondary school?

Any way, am off the soapbox!

I have a nice quiet evening planned as Nige has gone off to a wine and dine evening with work, where he gets to cook his own dinner with the help of a professional chef and then he gets the wine for free. I am rather hoping this chef can get Nigel off his sole specialty of A Le Beans on Toasty….

I live in hope.

February 12th, 2005

COO-EEE

Have spent the last two weeks feeling as though I have had a limb amputated! Nigel installed some new software and promptly lost 'windows'. The neighbours must think I've been having it away with the computer repair man the number of times he's been to the house! I felt really cut off from the 'real' world, and it was just me and the 'Septics'. My dear friend Kat has been staying with us for a week which has been wonderful. It peed down solidly the entire time she was here. She did say that a perk of being black was that she was going to lie to everyone and say the weather had been fabulous and no-one would query her lack of a tan!

We did laugh; the roof of the living room is flat so the rain thunders onto it. Between the rain and 10 hamsters running in their wheels we found ourselves yelling across three feet of space just to hear each other! I think she was in awe of the general din of our house anyway!

It was so lovely to have a good hearty belly laugh, it seems so long since I laughed until my massie ran! It's really hard to share a laugh here, the locals just don't have the same sense of humour and don't share the same terminology as us and it's not the same when you have to explain why something is so funny that your tea came out your nose! Buying funny cards here is impossible; the American humour is really obvious and banal. They are just so conservative. Sometimes the difference in terminology is really frustrating; recently I was going through the Yellow pages looking for a Ford garage. I tried garages, cars, car dealers and then eventually found it under Automobiles! The same thing happened trying to find some hairdressers, it's under Beauty Salons and Cinemas are under Theatres!

This week the boys went to a 9th birthday party which had a 'popstar' theme. A stretch limo picked them up from our house and took them into the city for dinner at the Hard rock Café where, they were given T shirts, studded bracelets and Drum gear!!!!!

What the bloody Nora will his parents do for him when he hits 18??? A private Learjet to Paris?

My boys will be nine soon and it will be a few mates out for a pizza and a movie for them!

I could do with a girls' night out, the women here don't seem to do this, they seem to socialise with their husbands and only at week-ends.

Maybe I need to start my Girls' nights in parties over here!

February 24th, 2005

ALLO, ALLO, ALLO

Not a good start to the week so things had better improve! Am quite sure there will not be any of you surprised to hear that I had the police here at the house at 4am on Wednesday/Thursday…

Leo has not been a good night time sleeper for a few weeks and I average getting up four times each night. Recently, things have got much worse and I have felt my patience ebbing away. Nigel had been away since the previous Friday and I was getting very little sleep. By 2:30am on Wednesday I lost the plot entirely, I yelled at poor Leo, slammed his door shut, went to my room and slammed my door shut, put cotton wool in my ears and tried to ignore his screaming!

Our bedroom is the only door that locks, and so for that reason I always leave the key in the outside of the door so that the kids will never be trapped in the room…

Well, by 4am Leo is still squawking and Abbie comes along to see what's going on. For some reason she turned the key, instead of the doorknob, and it only turned part way and therefore locked me in! I tried coaxing her to turn the key but she just couldn't do it, by this time Sam and Ben are awake too and Leo is still squawking at full volume. After 15 minutes of trying I had to talk Abbie into finding the Sheriffs phone number in the kitchen and get her to slide the number written on a piece of paper under the door. I felt a complete twit telling him what had happened and at one stage he was debating whether to bring the Fire Brigade!!

Whilst we waited for him to arrive, I could hear Ben trying to read a story to Leo whilst I ran round the bedroom hiding my knickers and bras. Thank-god I didn't have my rollers in and a facepack on!

The Sheriff eventually arrives with the bloody Nur Nur flashing. Four am and he has his top buttoned fastened and a perfect comb over.

Once he let me out, I had the humiliation of answering his questions whilst he filled out his incident form, painstakingly slowly!

Have now bought a book on toddlers with sleeping problems!

We have also had three unwelcome guests of the animal variety, ducks in the bloody pool! Whilst this might sound cute, I can assure you that ducky poop between your toes is not attractive! I asked the pool man for tips on how to get rid of them and he suggested an inflatable snake!

Talking of animals, I am a bit concerned that I have killed Rocky the Raccoon. Last week I bought a Mexican pork dinner for the kids and I to try. It was vile so we left it; unfortunately it was three days before I threw it out and put it in the wheelie bin. Somehow that clever Raccoon has learned to open the bin and the following morning there were bits of pork everywhere. That was four days ago, so, I have either fatally poisoned him or he is in his den with a very bad botty!

This week I went to get some Aromatherapy oils and really struggled to find somewhere that sold them. Eventually I found a shop with a limited collection, and I got talking to the shop assistant about how surprised I have been by the utter lack of any complimentary therapies available locally. She told me that this area of Marin County is THE most conservative place to live in the States and has the highest number of lawyers per head than any other state and, because of how litigatious the Californians are, then the Therapists simply cannot afford the insurance needed to practice here.

That did explain a lot, how very sad though. This is, after all, where the whole Hippie, free love movement started but just look at what it has become. This will obviously mean that I will not be able to work as a Reflexologist during our time here. It is just so conservative here it makes Maggie Thatcher look like a raving liberal! I seem to be surrounded by arrogant 'nouveau' riche people. The older generation seems to be much more relaxed and fun, although there are also very few old people about?

On the positive side the weather is improving once again. The geckos are back sunning themselves on the deck which means the slithery things will be out in force again. Yuck!

I found some great small bottles of sunscreen that attach to the kids' school bags. I am always paranoid about Abbie with her fair skin and red hair. I can buy it but will they remember to use it?

This week-end we are to hire a Winniebago for this summers' adventures!

O.M.G! I forgot to tell you that I have a confession to make. Remember I wrote that I had a dream about that dreadful shop owner in San Anselmo?.

Well, I did it. I exacted my revenge!

I got all dressed up, put on a big hat and dark sunglasses and went back to her shop. I carried a basket and casually added the most expensive items I could find.

As I walked about I secretly dropped stink bombs on the floor. Soon, the smell was overwhelming and customers began leaving the shop. I picked up a gorgeous mohair cardigan and went into the changing room where I left a fake dog turd under the chair!

When I had $1, 500 worth of goods I walked up to the counter where superbitch was standing, and said (in a really bad American accent)!

I'm real sorry but I just can't stand this awful smell any longer",

and then walked out of the shop leaving her to think she had just lost a huge sale!

Immature I know but it felt soo good!!

March 10th, 2005

A WEEK OF FIRSTS

The first, first of the week happened when I put the bins out for collection on Friday morning. I have, no doubt, mentioned before that Nige takes the wheelie bins down the drive because if I do it then the bin runs away with me due to how steep the drive is. I am the one that takes the smaller recycling bins down. It is our least favourite job to do, especially at night as there are no lights at all and there are deer, skunk and raccoons that startle you by running in front of you on the path.

The recycling bins are kept outside the backdoor, so I did my usual of picking them up only to find a snake had somehow got under the bucket and curled itself underneath. Well, I am surprised you could not hear my scream over in England!

Next, on my way to collect the boys from school I walk along the marshes. On this particular day I came across a young disabled bloke in a golf buggy. His back wheel had come off the path and had slipped into the marsh and so he was stuck. I spent the next 25 minutes trying to push, pull and lift him back onto the path but to no avail. I could not believe that people were just jogging, cycling or even walking past us and not one of them offered any assistance. In the end I had to go to the boys' school and commandeered the first three men I saw to come and help me! Disgusted is not the word. The poor man was embarrassed enough at a woman trying to lift his golf buggy but the fact that people just walked by beggars belief.

On Thursday we went off to Lake Tahoe. This is a ski resort in the Sierra Nevada mountains of Nevada State, which is the next state to California. It took us three and a half hours to drive there.

The scenery was stunning, and when we got there we found that our accommodation had been upgraded which was a bonus! That evening I had a massage in the hotel, imagine my total mortification to find out the masseuse was a bloke and an English one at that! I was too embarrassed to say anything. At one point he asked me to put my knees together and lift my hips off the bed, I thought he was going to give me a Smear test! By now I was having a fit of the giggles as all I could think of was that scene in James Herriot where he is shoulder deep up the cows' arse!

Not exactly the mellow relaxing massage I had hoped for!

The day we arrived there had been a huge snowfall and yet everyone was sitting outside the bars in the sunshine! The kids went to ski school to brush up on their snowboarding and ski-ing skills. They are all so confident now and are really good. The boys wanted to try a black run! They spent the morning in school and then Nige took them off for the afternoon before swapping to look after Leo so that I could go to ski-school. The less said about that the better.

The next day it snowed, and snowed, and snowed.

Despite this, Nige had promised the kids a last run before we headed back home. The weather was really bad, and, against my better judgment he said he would take the kids for just an hour. We were supposed to check out of the hotel by 11am. By 10:50 they still were not back and visibility out the hotel room window was zero. The snow had drifted right up to the first floor windows. All I could hear were the controlled avalanche explosions. I was starting to get quite anxious when Nige rang to say they were stuck up the mountain and he was having to bring the kids down one at a time as the lifts had closed. Thankfully he got them all down safely but we were both very tearful.

The journey back took us twelve long hours, the worst snow I have ever seen. We ended up sleeping in the car, but I was bloody thankful that I had insisted on stocking up on food and drinks for the journey. To keep our spirits up I sat in the back of the car with the kids singing'

"Always look on the bright side of life."

I asked them what had been the best part of the trip. They told me it was watching mummy pee on the side of the road and Dad driving forwards so the world could see mummys' bare bum! Mmm. I was just grateful I didn't pee in the back of my boots!

Next month we are off to Yosemite National Park and then, in May, to the infamous Santa Cruz boardwalk. From now on I am only doing sun, sand and sea…

Ski-ing at Squaw Valley, Lake Tahoe

March 22nd, 2005

A YEAR ON

Do you realize that tomorrow we will have been living here in botox bunny land for a year and that I continue to weigh more than 95 pounds and can still move all my facial muscles? Amazing.

This week will be Earthquake Drill Week. On Thursday there is to be a full evacuation procedure carried out at the schools. I will even receive a phone call telling me that there has been an Earthquake and to get to the school as quickly as possible. I rather assume that if there was a quake I would have also felt it? Anyway, no-one is allowed to drive onto the school grounds so I will have to hope the weather improves as it is a flipping long walk to school down that mountain for me and not one I fancy doing in this rain!

I have to provide photo ID before they will let me take the kids out of school. It has all been really well planned out, quite creepy though.

I actually got asked to go on a girlie night out at long last! Yippee.

Three of us went out for drinks so I got all dressed up, lippy, shaved my legs, the works. They took me to a nice wine bar and then we spent the rest of the night in a bloody biker bar playing pool!

It was an ok. night but they did seem to talk about school a lot. I tried to ingest a little humour by recounting my recent massage drama but of course they didn't understand 'smear' or the James Herriot reference so it fell a bit flat to be honest. Ho hum.

Nigel was off work for Good Friday and so I had assumed that the kids would be too. I was wrong though. Due to the fact that the majority of kids at the school are Jewish then no Christian holidays are celebrated so, like Christmas, Easter is a non event here. It is obviously not P.C.!

However, all the Jewish holidays are celebrated and have days off accordingly??

On Saturday we all went Whale watching at a lighthouse called Point Reyes to the west of here. The whole area is a National Park and is a big farming community. The farms all have numbers rather than names, dating back from when the land was divided up by the original settlers into lots.

The weather was perfect and the sea as calm as a mill pond. It was a pretty walk to the lighthouse and we were really lucky to see seven Grey Humpback Whales hugging the coast, within 20 minutes of arriving. The whales travel up the coast from Mexico where they go to breed and swim onto Alaska to feed. They were magical to watch, a real privilege to see.

We also saw lots of Elephant seals too. In August there are, apparently, Great White sharks to be seen in their breeding ground around the nearby Farrallon Islands. Naturally that got Sam and Bens' attention!

This morning (Sunday) we went off to an Easter party organized by Jenn, one of the mums in my Mothers Group. It was in a local park near the creek behind the boys' school. Jenn and her husband Ed had scattered 720 plastic eggs filled with sweets throughout the park! All the kids, about 50, were each given a basket to fill. Everyone brought some food so there was a hot ham roast, salad, pastas enough food for an army, all set up on tables with heaters and tents! Fabulous.

After the egg hunt was over there were games for the kids to play. As well as the usual egg and spoon race they played a game where the kids have to stand opposite a partner and play catch with a raw egg. Every time they catch it then they must take a step backwards until you have to throw the egg quite hard in order for it to reach your partner. You can imagine the state they were all in after three games!

Jenn and Ed organize this every year which is rather fun!

Next week-end is our trip to Yosemite or Yoz Mite as I call it. Hopefully this time we can avoid all fires and Earthquakes and get to see all the Waterfalls that had dried up last time we tried to see them!

So, Year two begins tomorrow, who knows what this one will bring. I'll keep you updated…

Point Reyes National Park

LIVING WITH THE BUNNIES
A BRITISH FAMILYS' EXILE TO MARIN COUNTY.

YEAR TWO

Contents

April 3rd, 2005

YOUR NEWS FROM THE BAY AREA

Nige has taken the boys to the 'movies' so Abbie, Leo and I have enjoyed a 'girlie' session tonight. We are ALL sporting bubble gum pink lippy and nail varnish! I actually resemble a cast member of the Rocky Horror Show.

On Thursday, at school, we had the planned Emergency evacuation drill. It was all spookily realistic, the sirens were kept on to maintain the air of urgency and all seemed to go as per plan. The schools here even have drills to teach the children what to do if someone enters the school premises with a gun. That one terrifies me, that this could even be a possibility, but America does have a history of nutters doing just that. It doesn't seem to make the powers that be change the law on guns here though. Guns really can be bought anywhere. There is a big sports chain shop here that sells them. I think that the law here says you can use a gun to protect your own property so many people here keep a gun in the house. Very scary.

I had a nice afternoon to-day. I was invited for 'tea' at the house of a woman who has a son at school with Sam and Ben. It was all very formal! She had obviously gone to enormous effort and served tea in a real china teapot and served butties on a silver platter with the crusts cut off! Next there were strawberries dipped in chocolate! It was posher than tea at the Ritz!

It was really kind of her to go to all the effort, it was not unappreciated and she seems really nice.

So, my social life is looking up, I have also been asked to go out with some girlies next Thursday. Whoo Hoo!

That's about all my news this week so I'll throw in some recent observations of life here in Botox bunny land.

Petrol or gas as the Yanks call it is so much cheaper, as are cars, but these are of considerable poorer quality than those found in the U.K.

There is a really high police presence, even on the shortest of journeys you are likely to see at least one squad car patrolling the local neighbourhoods.

I have never seen any kind of 'trouble' and never see gangs of youths hanging around.

There is no graffiti at all and there are no old people . . .? Could those two facts be connected?! Actually, I think once people turn 70 here a white van arrives and ships them off to live in Florida. Wrinkles ruin the Californian image of eternal youth, even if many pay for the effect!

Almost everything is cheaper except for Gas and Electricity. Now that was a shock! There is only one supplier for both so they obviously have the monopoly. We pay $400 to $600 a month for these!

Clothes are generally quite poor quality unless it's the big name brands. Apparently the Bush administrations have some agreement with China so the Standards are quite low. I actually wait till we come home to the U.K to buy our clothes!

Going back to the police, the local Sheriff (who is paid for by the residents of the Woodlands where we live) parks his squad car at one of the local schools each day. This way he gets to know all the local kids and their families. I think this is great, however, Abbie and her pals call him 'Sticky' as he always has jam down his shirt! Having had him in my boudoir at 4am I'll call him whatever he wants…

There really are many differences that you really wouldn't generally think of. I think I thought that because we (Brits and Yanks) all speak the same language then life would be quite similar but this just is not the case. The Marin people, here in this area, are really conservative and just, well, anal really.. Maybe it's because they are all descendants of the Missionaries that arrived during the Goldrush in the 1840's to ensure that people remained God fearing Christians whilst looking for the gold in them there hills!

Just a thought.

April 12th, 2005

SUPER DOOPER, WOT A BUNCH OF PARTY POOPERS!

I have been feeling very sorry for myself for the last two days. I have a brass band playing in my head and a gob that feels like I've licked the floor of the Sahara Desert.

On Sunday we had a party for Leo's 2nd birthday. Realising this was the first (and bloody last) party we have had here, and, expecting 25 people I went all out for it. Huge buffet, dozens of helium balloons, massive ice-cream cake, treasure hunts, piñata, pass the parcel, pin the tail on the donkey. You get the picture.

FOUR mums turned up, an hour late; one stayed 45 minutes before leaving to watch a Basketball game.

Thankfully there is always one reliable drunk at a party, well, two actually if you include me! On this occasion it was my friend Ruby whom I don't see as often as I would like to. It was Ruby's cabin we stayed at on the Russian river. I met her when we arrived at the open day for soccer. I went to pay the fees only to find they did not accept credit cards and I didn't have a cheque book with me. Ruby, who I had never set eyes on before that day, was in the queue behind me and immediately offered to pay my fees! I thought that was rather an amazing thing to do for a complete stranger. As it happened her daughter was on the same team as Abbie and we have been friends ever since. Anyway, Ruby and I kept up the party mood, played all the games and quaffed a hideous amount of wine.

By 9pm I was convinced I was the new Olga Corbett and had challenged all mine and her kids to a gymnastic competition. As a result I have been taking Ibuprofen tablets every four hours for the last two days!

Leo had a great time anyway, Ruby had very kindly bought him a drum set, and she is now minus one friend…

As for my girlie night out, well, it bombed as everyone was too tired!

This weeks interesting / boring facts about living in the United Stuck-up Arses

Although America is said to be the worlds' worst offender of polluting the ozone layer, the Californians are very 'hot' on recycling. Many shops have recycling bins immediately outside the shop doors as do the cafes and local parks. To recycle at home and to have household waste removed then you have to contact the local sanitation company and specify how big a bin you will require and then pay a monthly bill to have it all taken away. Obviously, the more you recycle the more you pay. Even a trip to the local tip will cost a minimum of $20. Having said that, I have not seen any fly tipping.

When you are paying for this service directly it certainly does make me more conscious of the way we dispose of waste. I now break up all cereal, shoe boxes, anything cardboard. All left over fruit and veg I throw over the fence into the 'wilderness' for the deer and Rocky (whose bottom has recovered, thankfully!) to eat. I do wish he would bring the bowl back, he is very rude. I put the food in a bowl for him and when he's finished eating he hurls it down the hill!

I have been very honoured this week. Apparently, I have been nominated as the coolest mum in the 5th grade as I listen to hip music like Usher and the Blackeyed Peas. What these kids don't realize is that I have to listen to this stuff in the car as I can't work the sodding C.D changer!

Next week-end we are off to Yoz Mite, no doubt it will be eventful!

Until we return.

April 17th, 2005

THE BARRETT FAMILY ON TOUR

We have spent the last few days hiking, swimming and cycling in the most beautiful setting of Yosemite National Park. We stayed in a lodge just outside the park. We hiked up to see some spectacular waterfalls and we went walking with a Park Ranger who took us on a Bear spotting trail. There are thought to be 300-500 black bears in the park. We cycled to see a lake called Mirror Lake where you can see the snow capped mountains reflected in the still surface of the lake. Just gorgeous.

The weather was in the upper 70's so it was really pleasant and it was really quiet, so no crowds. The scenery simply takes your breath away.

There is an old hotel called 'The Awahnee', named after the Indian tribe that once lived throughout the park. We sat outside on the hotel terrace for 'afternoon tea' just watching the kids play on the lawn and drinking in the smells and sounds around us. It is hard to put into words what the effect the place has on you; it really is the most beautiful place I have ever been to.

We spent the daytime exploring the park on bikes with Leo in a trailer on the back of Nigels' bike. In the evenings, once Leo was asleep, we left Nige to his books and we went off to swim in the indoor pool and spa. I love spending this time with the kids when we go away. We sit in the hotubs just chatting and laughing about anything at all.

So, we are back 'home' now and its only six weeks until the school summer holiday. O.M.G twelve weeks, I know I love my kids, but just not for that long!

I seem to live my life waiting for our week-ends away as they make up for the frustration I feel for the weeks in between! Our next planned trip is to Santa Cruz for a sand soccer tournament under the famous Boardwalk.

I am counting down the days already!

Yosemite National Park

April 28th, 2005

DE BITCH IS BACK!

Sometimes I really hate computers . . . not as much as I hate the Marinites but nearly!

We have had two 'power outages' or, power cuts as we know them. Both of which lasted five hours or more. The 2nd one blew out the modem for the computer so we have been unable to access the Internet and have been waiting for a new modem to be delivered. It's been like having a death in the family!

I seem to be on yet another anti Marin Campaign this week. Due to the lack of electricity on Friday night we all went out for dinner. I drove to a local town and went to the town public car park. There There was several parking several parking spaces cordoned off for valet parking, they like that here, it means you're a 'somebody' if you get your car valet parked. Personally, I think that they're just really crap at parking themselves. Anyway, I parked the Barrett Bus away from the cordoned off area and we all got out to go in search of a restaurant. No sooner had we got out than Little Hitler comes goose stepping over and demands my car keys! When I refused to give them to him he then asked me for $4! Naturally I refused to hand that over as well. A row ensued and he went off to phone the police and we went off to get dinner! When we returned two hours later Little Hitler had boxed me in! Not wanting to lose face and feeling really rather stroppy I got in the car and slammed it into reverse and shot backwards towards the nearest car! Well, you should have seen how fast that little Hitler ran to move all the cars out of my way! Cheeky buggers! So, I had a generally bad week last week, full of silly little incidents like this one. After a while they can really get you down.

I did, however, have a good night out on Saturday. We went into San Fran with some friends to a comedy club which was actually really good. I missed some of the jokes as he went a bit fast for me to follow, but, get this, there were signs everywhere saying that there was a limitation of two drinks per person! Naturally this meant I ordered two bottles of wine. The show lasted for one hour exactly and then you were chucked out for the show to be repeated to a new audience. We were home by 10:30pm!

I feel I have now ostracized myself at school for not being bullied into this cringe worthy 'Teachers' appreciation day' malarkey. It is getting ridiculous with demands for flower, herbs, money, poems and embroidered frigging bookmarks and then asking me to wait on the teachers whilst they ate a meal cooked by the parents!

Times this three fold and I'd had enough of this arse licking contest and sent out an email stating that I did not wish to compete and that each of my kids' teachers would receive a handmade card (made by kids, not me!) and some nice smellies or similar. They are all making Voo Doo dolls of me as I type...

The children all have Star Tests this week, equivalent to the CAT tests, I think. I have had to provide drinks and snacks for the whole bloody class. Poor Ben has been stressed out as he 'only' got 95% for the last maths test and that would be a fail!

Abbie has got 'Career Day' to-day. I suggested that she says she wants to be a mortuary assistant as there are no queues for lunch and no one to talk about you behind your back!

As for International news, it was interesting to see a new pope appointed. 75% of the Catholic population is African or Latino so the Vatican appoints a German pope? Nice to see the masses being well represented I think. The only way we hear of any news other than that about America is via the internet. Naturally the Americans are only interested in what's happening in America and so; therefore, do not report on any where else! Unless, of course, it involves out very own Monarchy and then they are drooling over all footage.

That's my bitch for the week over with!

May 7th, 2005

THIS WEEKS MEMOIRS FROM A BRIT ABROAD

I am almost ashamed to admit that we have had a really good week! The hot weather has at last kicked in; the kids come home from school and jump in the pool. I just love watching them all splash about. If I'm lucky Leo has a nap and then I join the others in the water. The temperature of the water is 82 degrees so it's like getting into a warm bath. I have enjoyed the pool most about being here, the kids are now really confident in the water and swim well, which is just as well as this pool shelves rather quickly!

On Tuesday I was invited to someones' house who was hoping to start up an International Mothers Group for all local ex pats. It was wonderful, there were 15 of us at this meeting and we came from all over the world, including, Lebanon, Germany, Sweden, Ethiopia, Czech Republic, France and four of us from Good old Blighty!

They were a great bunch of girls and we all got on well and plan to meet up once a month on our own and once a month with children. I really love the idea of my kids mixing with lots of different cultures; I think there is no better way to prevent racism.

This week, in the school newsletter I was quite shocked to get the usual drivel from the head but this time the topic was paedophilia. Here in California they have what is known as Megan Law which enables Joe public to log onto a website that lists all known and registered sex offenders in your area. This information includes names, address, photo ID and details of the crimes they committed. Apparently, in some states a sign can be put up outside the offenders' home. As a parent I wholly agree with the register but I think the sign outside the house is an infringement on human rights but where then do you draw the line or should there even be a line?

There are 63,000 registered sex offenders here in California. Do remember that California is five times bigger than the entire U.K.

On a lighter note, we attended three parties on Saturday! It was great fun except I couldn't have a drink as I was doing all the driving as Nige is away again! We went to a pool party first and then in the afternoon on to a BBQ where I met a nice English girl from

Gerrards Cross! She has been here with her hubby and three kids for a year more than us and still finds it tough at times so we had a good bitch and moan!

I have had only one 'Fionaism' this week that involved a teacher from Abbies' school. I was parked in the pick up line, the boys each had a friend with them and the four of them were standing outside the car (too hot in it!) and were playing with light sabers. They are all taking part in a school talent show and were re-enacting a scene from Star Wars. I saw in my rear view mirror Attila the Hun approaching for a fight. She was SO aggressive and rude to the four boys that I had to step out the car and pointed out they were with me, I was the person responsible for them, not her, and that it would me and me alone that would discipline them if I thought they were misbehaving but seeing as they most definitely were not then I failed to understand her interference.

I was furious, it is funny how if someone was aggressive to me like that and I was alone I would be a blubbering wreck but be like that to my kids and all of a sudden I'm Braveheart!

Grrrrr!

May 15th, 2005

WILDLIFE ON MOUNT TAM

So, we have Rocky the Raccoon who lives under the deck, hundreds of Geckos in the garden walls, Daphne and Daffy Duck in the pool, snakes in the recycling bins and mountain lions higher up the hill, but, by far the cutest guest was left on the front doorstep last Friday morning.

A tiny fawn!

I opened the front door to go to school and there she was, curled up on the front door mat! I rang the local wildlife centre who informed me that this is quite common! Apparently, mummy Bambi does not take the new baby out foraging with her for the first few days. What she does is leave the baby somewhere safe and camouflaged early in the morning and then returns to get the baby at twilight.

I can only presume this was a first time mother seeing as she left her baby on the doorstep of a house with four kids and a dog!

The house is a greyish colour and the door mat is beige but I would hardly call it good camouflage!

She stayed on the doormat for 12 hours and hardly moved. I put water out for her and took lots of pictures and she just pretended not to see us.

We took care not to touch her so Mum would not smell humans on her.

As for Raffy Roo? He totally ignored her, carefully stepped over her, no sniffing, nothing!

When Nigel got home, we set up the camcorder on the steps and filmed mum when she came back for her. It was lovely, she made a soft sound and Bambi was up and trotting down the stairs to greet her.

The deer community has obviously forgiven me for the one that died in the garden.

That was the pleasant wildlife encounter of the week. The other encounter was vile. The boys had some friends over to play and had gone off over the fence into the Wilderness to explore. After a while I saw Sam run into the kitchen and come out with a bulky tee shirt, not a good sign as any mother of boys will tell you.

A short time later all the boys came running over to me, Sam holding a Tupperware bowl with a lid on.

"Look what we found mum," he says

I gingerly lift the lid, determined not to show fear, which would send the boys into whoops of laughter...

Inside the box was a very cross, pincher waving scorpion.

Well, I could have beaten Fatima Whitbread in the Olympic disc throwing with how far I hurled that box and its content!

I did have what is now referred to as a 'Fionaism' last week.

We were a little late for school on the day we found Bambi. As I was waiting at the traffic lights, there was a middle aged man behind me on a motorbike. Once the light was green, I put my foot down a bit, (do bear in mind I drive a Sherman tank, with a max speed of 40mph) when I hear shouting from behind us. Thinking that the boot or a door is open I look in the rear view mirror and the guy on the bike is puce in the face and screaming obscenities at me! The next thing is, he has pulled along side our car and is making the 'L' gesture on his forehead and was almost dribbling venom! Abbie informed me he was calling me a 'loser'. The silly git obviously thought I had been trying to race him off at the lights! All I could do was laugh, what a sad, sad man. I will now make a point of waving gaily to him each morning we see him.

The drivers here really are unbelievable. I got so cross I made two signs for the back window of my car. One is a picture of a hand with the middle finger sticking up with the caption

Honk me, get the finger.

This being due to the locals being so aggressive that they hit the horn for a few seconds for anything.

The other sign says

I'll decide if it's safe to pull out, not you.

Abbie keeps removing them!

Yesterday we finally managed to walk to the top of Mount Tam. It was really hard work but the views were worth the climb. We could see right over the bay to San Francisco and across the East bay to Berkeley. At the very top there is a lookout post that the fire services use to look out for fires on the mountain. In October the fire service put on a pancake breakfast for anyone willing to make the trek to the top.

This morning we went to a fantastic outdoor Farmers market in the next town north of here called San Rafael. It is held in the car park of a striking blue roofed building that is the Jewish Community centre and was designed by Frank Lloyd Wright.

There were hundreds of stalls selling fruit, flowers, honey, clothes, all sorts of local produce. There were food stands dotted all over with mouth-watering smells wafting down every aisle.

For the kids, there were pony rides and jumpees, which is what they call Bouncy castles here.

I got chatting to a very nice guy which does not often happen here. We have found that the Americans from the East coast are a whole lot more open minded and friendly. This could be due to them having more contact with Europeans as it is now so cheap to fly into New York from Europe. I am beginning to wish that Nigel had taken up a job offer on Wall Street!

We ended the day at a local Sushi bar for dinner. All very authentic, or so I assumed, until Nige pointed out that every single member of staff was actually Chinese...

Bambi left on our doorstep

May 21st, 2005

LIFE IN LA LA LAND, HOME OF THE BOTOX BUNNY

An interesting start to the week, whilst my oldest darlings were playing Basketball outside, a row erupted between Abbie (Narky knickers) and Sam (Mr. Attitude), the result being Mr. Attitude threw the ball at Narky Knickers' head who then made a big, big fuss and was up in the night complaining of a headache.

This was, therefore, our first trip to an American hospital, which is, thankfully, only a five minute drive from here. It was very impressive, very clean and really efficient. We have medical insurance through Nigels' job as it is unbelievably expensive to be ill here. Narky knickers was seen within half an hour of arriving, five minutes after the Doctor was finished I was signing the bill! $150 to be told she was fine but should be kept off school for the day!

Poor Mr. Attitude was very worried about her and wrote a letter of apology and spent his pocket money on a pretty pair of earrings for her.

Lovely gesture, shame her ears aren't pierced though!

We had our week-end in Santa Cruz and I think I got on everyones' nerves! I don't know why I go to beaches because I hate sand and how it gets into your butties and in your knickers and round the lid of your drinking bottle.

Nigel makes me try to not moan for the first hour so the kids get some enjoyment. I sit and sulk on my towel and no-one is allowed within three feet of me, I even have a pop up tent so that I can keep my food and drinks away from everyone elses!

It took us two hours to drive there and ended up looking like an exact replica of Blackpool pleasure beach. Vile!

The hotel, which I admit I booked, was on a main road. The pool was more or less on the pavement and there was a 24hour off license next door. Think of all those crime novels you have read where the victim is found dead in the bath of some sleazy motel that smells of stale pee and damp and you get the idea of our week-end accommodation!

Saturday was warm and sunny, Nige gave me 'the' lecture and I promised to not whinge for the first hour.

I must say I was pleased to see that at the top of all sets of stairs leading onto the beach there were foot taps to wash your feet before putting your shoes back on.

The kids all managed to find a team to play on and I went for a stroll along the waters' edge. My ears quickly picked up an English accent and I hunted down the source. Turned out she was a London lass who lives near us and her son is in Sam and Bens Year. Cannot believe I haven't met her before, there are not exactly a lot of English people at school! We had a good old moan and gripe about the bunnies which I find soothes the soul, plus I happen to be very good at it.

Remember last year when I mentioned about this 'select' soccer team that the boys were invited to tryout for? We decided it was too much for us to manage and so we didn't tell the kids. Well, there was a select team there whose coach saw Sam and Ben play, he came over to us and immediately asked that the boys be allowed to join his select team. We are now having the life plagued out of us by the boys!

I managed not to whinge too much although I did insist everyone remove all clothing inside the hotel room door and shower straightaway so that the nasty sand did not get into the sheets. Hate that.

That evening we found a Curry restaurant

Yipeeeeeeee!

We gorged ourselves disgustingly and gleefully having not had the joy of eating a good curry in a very long time; the motel room sure didn't smell of just damp and pee the next day!

We woke up on Sunday morning (Mothers Day) to pissing rain. I looked appealingly to Nige and the kids and told them they must be ruddy joking about playing soccer on the sand in torrential rain. Alas not, off we went after a slap up brekkie at a real American Diner.

I moaned for SIX hours, I was cold, wet and the feel of the sand on my feet was horrible. I refused to let Leo out of his pushchair and thankfully he fell asleep for hours. Strangely, it is impossible to buy pushchairs with rain covers or, even more bizarrely with sun parasols. I have so many people ask me where I get them from.

Eventually Nige could suffer me no longer and plonked me in a greasy spoon restaurant at the end of the pier with a pot of tea, a plate of chips and my book!

You have never seen anything more depressing than a game of sand soccer in the pouring rain. Half of the teams had more sense and had not even shown up. Of course, our three were right up for it despite being purple with cold!

By 4pm I had had enough and insisted on coming home. As it was Mothers day we stopped at a local restaurant for dinner, we looked like a right family of pikeys. Creased clothes, sand in our hair and stuck to our legs and me with a plastic necklace with animal charms on it with matching bracelet and earrings, mothers' day gifts and worn with pride!

The weather forecast for the rest of the week is perfect, so I will catch up on the washing.

There's bloody sand in everything.

May 30th, 2005

BITS N' BOBS

Have just got back from the Fat Bastard gym and opened a chilled bottle of Pinot Grigio!

It has been incredibly hot to-day; even I only managed to sit outside for 45 minutes before scuttling back inside to the air conditioning!

Abbie took part in a concert this week which had a Beatles' theme to it. It sounded rather odd, all these classics sung in an American accent! The kids were very impressed when I told them I use to live in Liverpool and that my middle name is Michelle after the song Michelle my Belle. On Sunday we went to a local flower and food festival where there was a model / acting agent who asked the kids if they would like to go for some castings . . .

Abbie was right in there signing on the dotted line but, if it doesn't involve a ball then it holds no interest for my boys!

This week the boys are off camping, have a soccer tryout tomorrow and a pool party on Friday afternoon!

I thought I would give you some general tid bits of local history.

For those of you who enjoy reading American crime novels then you have most likely heard of San Quentin jail. This is a huge prison built here in 1852; it is actually a very impressive piece of architecture and sits on prime real estate land overlooking the Bay. We can just about see the prison from our deck. In the first apartment we lived in the kids' use to play on the small beach beneath one of the watch towers! It is the only prison in California where inmates can be executed and it has recently announced it is to build a new death row to house 1,300 inmates. In doing so, this will double the number of inmates awaiting execution!

Since America re-introduced the death penalty in 1978 there have been 11 executions, 35 have died of other causes and the rest are awaiting appeals. This rather makes me wonder why the courts still pass the death sentence and is it really an effective deterrent and is it financially or ethically worth it?

The latest addition to death row is Scott Peterson, accused (and found guilty) of murdering his pregnant wife and fetus and throwing them into the Bay.

Every time you get on the ferry at Larkspur Landing to travel to the city the boat passes the prison. Often, the inmates are in the exercise yard and wave to the boats as they pass. Leo loves waving to the nice men in the Orange outfits!

Despite local pressure to get rid of the prison it is unlikely to close as the County is paid a vast amount of money just for having it here. This new extension is thought to be costing $220,000,000 to build. The prison authorities claim this is cheaper than giving the inmates Life without parole!

Housing.

Marin County is considered to be the second most expensive place to live outside of Westchester, New York. There are more than 4,000 estate agents or Realtors as they are called here. Most of these are chasing resale homes as there is a No New Build policy. If you want a new house you need to first buy an old one and then get planning permission to knock it down and then rebuild a new house! The Realtors charge a whopping 6% per sale and so don't have to sell too many properties in a year to make some serious cash!

A bungalow near us is in an uninhabitable condition and yet is on the market for $2.5 million just because it is on a flat lot and not on a hill.

Speaking of which, I have been shopping for quotes to have our windows cleaned. $450 was the average price! Most people have them done just once a year as it involves serious money and scaffolding being erected.

It must surely have been a man who thought to build a city on the side of a frigging hill!

Now at least I understand why most houses are built with a large overhang above the windows. It is to protect the glass from getting dirty from the elements.

I got the ladders out and did what I could of ours!

San Quentin Jail.

June 11th, 2005

CHAV NEWS FROM THE U.S.A

Now I understand what all this talk of 'chavs' is about. Nigel downloaded a documentary by the ultimate Chav bint, Julie Burchill, which explained the whole concept so now I am in the know!

Interestingly, the sociologist on the documentary was my old Sociology teacher from college, Bev Skeggs. I remember her telling us about something that happened to her when she was doing her own University Thesis on Communism. Bev had gone to her local library and checked out the maximum number of books allowed on her chosen subject matter. A few days later she had a knock on her door from 'Big Brother', our eyes are everywhere, asking lots of questions about her reading material!

I am beginning to comprehend much of what she taught us about how things are not always as they seem. For example, Americans view America as the land of the free and yet here in Marin I find it so repressed, I can almost understand what drives a person to 'lose the plot' and go on a mad gun rage.

This is the most black or white culture you can imagine and I am not talking race issues. There is no room for individuality or self expression or any kind of flexibility.

To-day, for example. We drove to a nearby state park called China Camp. The kids were really excited and wanted to take their bikes. Once you have parked the car there are no more roads. We set off on our bikes along a coastal path. Out of nowhere appears the Sheriff

"You kids ain't wearing any safety helmets and that there is against state regulation number blah, blah, blah. I have the right to inform you that you may be prosecuted under state law blah, blah, blah."

He was rigid and escorted us back to the car where we gave up and drove home.

Infuriating.

It is so frustrating, you can put your dog in a dress, take it into most shops and there are doggie bakeries and hotels to cater to the needs of your pampered pooch, but hells bells if you think you're allowed to treat it like a dog and let it off the lead anywhere for a run, then think again!

Each town has a dog park with a small enclosure and this is the only place your dog can be a flaming dog!

AGGGHHHHHHH!

I had one of lifes' defining moments this week too. It was 'Open Evening' at Abbies' school. She was dressed as a cowgirl (?), Leo was all clean and Sam and Ben looking smart. As I was about to open the front door Nigel rang to say he was stuck in a lift 29 floors up, Leo announced "I poohed," and Abbie screamed there was a snake on the living room floor.

Turn the clock back 15 years and I would have chosen to be a nun.

If Nigel ever manages to get out the lift then tomorrow he is flying to Los Angeles, staying at The Beverly Wilshire Hotel and is attending a party at the Playboy Mansion.

Hate him.

As for me, I have 14 boys coming for a pizza and a sleepover for Sam and Bens 9th birthday party. I can hardly wait. Not.

At least I have a girlie night planned and have invited a posse of girls over for chilli and wine.

Hopefully some of them will have the good manners to show up this time…

I did manage to restrain myself this week from being incredibly sarcastic. One of the Mums'phoned, whose son has been invited to Abbie's party, with a list of questions she wanted answering before allowing 'precious' to attend. Get this, she wanted to know:

1) How many kids were attending and what were their ages?

2) What fire precautions were there in the house?

3) Would I be serving cake?

4) How exactly did I plan to keep the kids occupied and would they be playing games

and my favourite,

5) What would be the ratio of adults to children?

Do remember this was a party for a 12 year old, so, before answering I took a deep breath and politely answered all her questions in a calm reasonable (ish) voice. When what I wanted to say was the kids would be hanging out doing their thing in Abbies Crib, condoms would be readily available, but I had asked that the kids not use the family silver when 'doing lines' or lighting the 'pipes' and to ensure they put the empty beer and wine bottles in the recycling buckets!

Purleese!

June 17th, 2005

CAN I GO TO BED YET?

Well, Abbie certainly had a Birthday she will never forget!

I woke up on the 15th at 5 a.m. to the sound of a nearby helicopter. After 20 minutes I gave up sleeping and dragged myself downstairs. The helicopter and a police plane were circling over the house!

I immediately put the TV on to see the local news and soon heard that a convict had escaped from San Quentin jail! By 7am the school phone tree was in full swing and we were called to say there would be no school until the convict was caught.

Apparently, he had jumped out of an ambulance whilst en route to the local hospital and had run through the school grounds and was thought to be hiding in the Marshes behind the school.

He was picked up TWELVE hours later . . . just how difficult could it have been to find a man wearing only a pair of orange shorts, covered in tattoos and handcuffs?!

The next thing, Ben shouts,

"Earthquake"

and the Tsunami warning siren went off!

It was total chaos; the police evacuated more than 4,000 people in 30 minutes which is amazing. Thankfully the tsunami did not happen.

It was all rather exciting.

On Friday night we had Abbies Academy Awards party with 30 kids dressed as their favourite movie or pop star. You know your kids are growing up when they ask for Teriyaki chicken, sushi and Caesar salad for party food! Whatever happened to a bit of quiche and a sausage on a stick?

The night went really well, I had decorated the basement room in black wrapping paper and then suspended gold stars from the ceiling. There were awards for the best dressed Stars. We found a D.J by putting posters up around the local college offering $200 for a DJ to host the night. The guy who came was great, he does the hospital radio and had all the gear plus he kept the party under control. Naturally I was banned from going into the room!

The next day, after it taking me four hours to clean up the basement Abbie went for her first audition with this acting / modeling agency. She got through a day of auditions and was one of three out of 500 who auditioned that was then offered a place at Stage School. She had to do the auditions in front of some bigwigs from L.A. We don't call her a drama Queen in our house for nothing!

Actually I had to admire her; I would rather have my teeth pulled with no anaesthetic then do what she did.

So, we now have a true 'lovey darling' air kisser in the family!

I promised them I would be the realist and keep her grounded!

This afternoon we went off to Toys R Us so the kids could spend their birthday money. Sam bought an inflatable jet ski for the pool and Ben, despite being 'cool' at nine bought a cuddly Giraffe.

Ah, bless!

So, the last day of school was Friday, I now have 11 weeks, five days and 17.5 hours till they go back. Tomorrow I am cooking dinner for 15 for the International mothers' group. After that I am hibernating for 11 weeks, four days and 17.5 hours...

Just want to say thank-you for all the recent emails. They all had the same theme running through them,

Dear Fiona, please don't return to the U.K. this summer as we are having a heat wave.

Thanks for that.

June 22, 2005

HELLO FROM THE DOG HOUSE

I am writing from Raffys' outdoor kennel which I anticipate will be my main abode for the foreseeable future. Abbie and I were all set to compete in a fun run this morning. We set off, her with a bottle of mineral water and me with a bottle of Rioja, got to the start point only to discover the race was yesterday. Ouch!

To say she was a little cross with me would be an understatement. I now have to find another one; there is a really good website here that lists all major fun runs / walks nationwide.

Other than that, Nigel returned from his 'business, my arse, trip'. He came back with lots of presents. . Playboy magazines, playboy calendar, playboy keyrings and, oh yes, hundreds of photo's of him with his arms around the Playmates. He happily told me that while it looks like they are wearing bikinis' they are, apparently, utterly starkers except for body paint. How tasteful.

Think I'll put him in the bloody dog house.

We went for a tour of Leos' new Montessori nursery this week. I don't know how I kept my face straight with the teacher. She talked in a little girl voice and had the children twirling around whilst pretending to pluck colours out the sky. Last time I saw people doing stuff like that was on the acute psychiatric unit at Sefton General Hospital! The teacher then told me that she too has a son whose name is . . . True! No flipping' wonders kids in America divorce their parents. Alright, I know that's a bit of a cheek coming from someone whose son has the middle name of Z. . ., no, sorry, cannot bring myself to type it and chuck it into the public forum. That was Nigels' fault anyway and a perfectly good reason for a divorce!

I took 12 boys out to the movies to see the new Star Wars movie for Sam & Bens birthday. The queues were unbelievable. The movie theatre is the one that George Lucas uses to premiere all of the Star Wars movies; it is a small Art Deco type building in a residential area. He has recently paid for it to be nicely refurbished. It has only one screen, it is cash only to get in and has a tiny shop that sells very little!

I was rather embarrassed that I had told all the parents that the film finished an hour before it actually did! I did take them all for a coffee at a great nearby bookshop as compensation. The shops here don't open until 10 / 11 am and so are open much later. Unless of course you like to eat later then you are scuppered as all the restaurants close at 9:30 pm!

In the news this week, there have been a lot of protests to get Arnie out of office, he has closed SO many schools and the teachers are out on the picket lines. There have been requests for Californians to boycott shopping at the Gap Stores, a San Francisco family started this chain, as they have been largely funding Arnies' campaign to become Governor.

One thing I do have to say about the Yanks is that I do believe that their education system, locally anyway, is somewhat better than our own. I have noticed here that the teachers whilst being generally young are highly motivated and take obvious pleasure in their work. Sam has an inspirational teacher who has just done wonders for his confidence.

There does not appear to be a problem with discipline, whilst being very strict they are also very fair and the kids seem to genuinely want to please them and succeed at school.

In Abbies' school kids are given the teachers' email address and are encouraged to email the teacher with any homework queries. The majority of the teachers offer extra tuition outside of school too, so there seems to be a lot of dedication. From what I can gather the teachers' pay seems similar to those of teachers in the U.K. so I wonder why we don't see that same general level of dedication and commitment from our own teachers? The Government can hardly be to blame because the teachers get even less support from them here than they do at home.

Food for thought...

June 28th, 2005

I IS HERE IN DE HOUSE

A pleasant week in the Barrett household. I have even had a bit of a social life! I went on a girlie night out for dinner and then we ended up at that bloody biker bar again! It is really weird, it is supposed to be a biker bar and it is really scruffy but is full of people in suits and ties playing Shuffleboard and Pool. It is the only place open after 10pm so everyone heads there after a night out.

We also went to a pool party at the house of the girl who invited me for 'afternoon tea'. I have now named her Queenie and she just loves to entertain! She has a beautiful home with a large pool and hot tub. She had cooked a Thai dinner for all the adults and ordered a Pizza for the kids. She is a lawyer for the American equivalent of British Telecom. It was a very relaxing afternoon for most people but I spent the whole time following Leo around as there was no fence around the pool!

Yesterday we spent the day at home lounging around our own pool and chasing the ducks off! Last week I had bought a cover to go over the pool thinking that would keep Daphne and Daffy off the water but no, they just sit and crap on that as well! The kids all look so healthy and tanned. After a week of intense heat everything has turned from Green to Yellow. Each State has a nickname, Florida is known as the Sunshine State and California is known as the Golden State. This has nothing to do with sand or sun but is due to the fact that all the habitation snuffs it in the heat and turns Yellow! As for the wildlife, we have a few Turkeys in the garden at the moment. We did toy with the idea of freezing Christmas dinner early but neither of us could do the deed. Ugly buggers they are.

The kids have now finished school for 12 weeks. I am hoping that now we know more people then it won't feel quite so long! I have been busy booking them into various camps which seems to be the thing to do here. Naturally with my lot there are a lot of Sports camps as well as some creative ones.

This week's observations

Cars are much cheaper but seem to be of poorer quality

Petrol or gas as they say here is much cheaper – I pay $2.49 a litre.

Car tax is cheaper but the road conditions are generally rather poor.

No such thing as an MOT here and you see a lot of junky cars.

15 is the legal age to drive which would explain the high mortality rate on the roads and why the Americans are appalling drivers!

Mobile phone use whilst driving is legal.

July 3rd, 2005

A WEEK-END IN HIDING

Viva Glorious Britain, God Save the Queen, up to anything British!

Naturally we won't be saying any of these things as tomorrow is when the Yanks celebrate their independence from us lot. We, therefore, use sign language to communicate if we leave the house!

It is a bit like Jubilee every year, out comes all the flags and the bunting, lots of street parades and parties and firework displays.

The girl who cuts my hair made me laugh, yesterday, after asking me all about England and was Mongolia north of England (no, honestly, she really did!) She then asked me what we were doing to celebrate Independence Day. Doh!

She makes me laugh, she puts me under the Octopus dryer and then she nips over the road to the clinic for her botox shots to her forehead and then comes back to check my hair is dry!

The whole hairdressing experience is very different here. Each salon rents out the chairs to individual hairdressers so when you make an appointment you phone the individual hairdresser on her mobile. She will be the one that washes, cuts and dries your hair. There is no cup of coffee and the salons are quite basic although the second one I went to did have a manicurist there too.

Neither do they seem to attend shows or competitions to keep updated on latest styles.

I was tempted to reply that we spent all year making little effigies of irritating Americans and on the 4th we stuck pins in them all.

I had another good week actually; my friend Ruby came over for tea with her girls. She has recently bought a Maltese Terrier and gave it the name Harry bloody Potter. The poor mutt arrived in a carpeted Holdall bag; it has two raincoats, a life jacket and a frigging cashmere jumper!

For tomorrow Ruby has only bought the poor animal a star-spangled hat, a red frilly skirt with a matching jacket. I kid you not.

I wouldn't mind but this is my 'normal' American friend!

Whilst we are on the subject of dogs my own poor Raffy is currently being called 'Gaylord' due to going to the groomers and coming out wearing a bright bandana and they had trimmed his eyelashes so that they fanned his face! Poor thing looks totally ashamed of himself. He needs a dollop of fresh fox poo to roll in to get his dignity back.

I have now joined a local book club! No, I am not turning into a nerd; there are six girls who meet once a month in a bar (that was the deciding factor!). They were a really good giggle and took me to an English pub where I had my first pint of Boddingtons in a year.

Bliss, tasted like Amber nectar. Mmmmmmmmmmmm

It was like being on the Costa Del Crime, full of English and Irish looking like lobsters with the walls decorated with footie scarves… fanbloodytastic!

I introduced the girls to the English pint and insisted they drank it down in 10!

On Friday night Nigel went off into the city at midnight to watch the 2nd British Lions game in some dingy pub on the wrong side of town. Last week he parked in McDonalds next door and had the car towed away! He has been SO incensed by Woodcocks line up that he has emailed him expressing his frustration! He is currently top of the Fantasy Rugby league which I find amusing, but there are probably only two other people playing!

To-day we went into San Fran to an exhibition I wanted to see called 'The Universe Within' which is an amazing display of cadavers which have been plasticized to show the internal structures of the body. Each exhibit is stripped down to show each system individually.

One exhibit in particular is thinly sliced from head to toe like a total body MRI scan showing a detailed cross section through the whole body.

The kids had mixed feelings, Abbie was totally engrossed and the boys were swaying between morbid fascination and being totally grossed out.

Leo just thought they were all characters out of Star Wars...

As for Nigel he walked in, walked out and stayed in the foyer!

Tomorrow we are off to the town of Corte Madera to watch the parades and have a picnic in the park. Obviously we will put on our best Yankee accents although we may have to gag Nigel for that bit.

I cooked a roast Chicken to-day which got me thinking of all the things I miss. One being proper Bisto gravy powder not those nasty granules you add boiling water too. I am not a cake lover but the kids really miss Angel layer cake or Battenberg cake. Custard is another; personally I find the stuff reminds me of cold vomit. I really miss our bread! Here it is all called sour dough and tastes like vinegar. Yuck!

Feel all queasy now...

July 11th, 2005

NINE MORE WEEKS TO GO...

Firstly can I say that you have all been in my thoughts since the bombings in London and I am glad you are all safe. I know one of you was in the heart of it all and it must have been terrifying. One of Nigels' colleagues in London lost a relative in the bus explosion.

The fucking locals here. One of them had the nerve to say to me "Oh, now the Brits must have an idea of what we went through with 9/11"!

I curtly replied that the older British generation had suffered through the Blitz and the younger generation had experienced more than 25 years of terror like this courtesy of the IRA, who were largely funded by Irish American sympathizers . . .

McDonalds we've got bombs for you.

Oh, they make me so cross at times!

On a lighter note! Abbie and I had a lovely girlie bonding day on Saturday. We went off to one of the many local nail salons for a pedicure and manicure. This is really cheap to do here and they give you a fantastic 20 minute massage to die for!

Abbie also had a modeling audition this afternoon which was very exciting for her.

After her acting 'lovey' classes we headed off to the beach, please do not think that they are like what you see in Hello Magazine, cos they're not! You don't bother even going to the beach until after 2pm when you can be sure the fog has lifted, you always take a jumper and never swim in the sea because of the sharks! That said we had a cracking game of rounders that left me knackered! On the way home we stopped at an English pub called the Pelican. Apparently it was shipped brick by brick from England and now sits on the main road to the beach.

This week the kids have been to an education Camp, so far so good with not too much complaining! On Friday Nigel and I have been invited to a Ballroom dancing party at the home of some friends. Apparently they have hired caterers and a professional dance teacher and a barman. Sounds fun!

The weather is set to hit the 100 degree mark which is even too hot for me.

Nige is still feeling morose following the final defeat of the Lions.

As for those of you asking about Nigels job. He does enjoy it, the hours are flexible and he has a short beautiful commute across the Bay each day. His colleagues are not particularly sociable though, there are no lunches out. A secretary takes the lunch order each day and they tend to eat in the board room or in their own offices. I think the Americans generally take work very seriously and have only two weeks off a year. Having said that he does leave home later in the mornings and is often home by late afternoon on a Friday which we never had working in London. Parking at the ferry is free and the cost of crossing on the ferry is minimal so we don't have the astronomical travel costs that we had when commuting from Hemel to London each day. We paid £2, 500 a year just to park his car at the railway station, not including the rail fare for a crap service. This week we are celebrating Raffy being five years old and me having been off the ciggies for a year!

July 17th, 2005

LUAU GREETING TO YOU ALL

Incase you were all wondering where the Yanks go on holiday when only 30% of them have a passport the answer is Hawaii. Just about every person I have spoken to since school finished has either been or is about too!

To-day we have been to a Luau party at Queenies' house. We all had to wear a traditional Hawaiian costume which basically consists of jeans and a really nasty shirt for men and a grass skirt and coconuts for a woman. There was no shop that sold coconuts in my boob size so I got out of that one!

In true Queenie style the whole pool area was decked out as a Tiki bar and the main drink of the day was the 'Matai', I am not entirely sure what else is in them except for vast amounts of Rum! There were six families there and the kids stayed in the pool the whole day as the weather got into triple figures!

On Saturday the boys were at a friends house for a sleepover, Abbie was staying at a friends cabin on the Russian river so it was just Nigel, Leo and myself for the night! It felt strange to have a quiet house. We did consider a night of wild passionate abandon but settled on dinner out, early to bed with a cup of tea and a good book. Best nights' sleep I've had in years!

Before we went out Ruby came over with a birthday cake to celebrate Harry Potters 1st birthday! Thankfully she had resisted the urge to buy him some bling bling tiara to mark the occasion. I swear to God if she were in England I'd have to report her to the RSPCA.

Nigel and I really enjoyed that Ballroom Dancing party. It was a fabulous night, everyone was dressed up, there was a bar man mixing cocktails, Californians all have wet bars in their homes and just love these cocktails!

These friends live on the mountain, further up than us. They had put tables all around the deck overlooking the Bay. On each table there was a candle and a rose. It was beautiful and the food scrummy.

After we had eaten, we were led into the main living area which has a wooden floor and huge fireplace at one end. We had an hours dance lesson in the Waltz, Samba and the Salsa with a lovely teacher who was as camp as a row of tents!

After the lesson we bopped the night away or at least until 11 p.m. when people started leaving. What made the night for me was meeting an English bloke called Adam and his wife. He was a broad Mancunian and ardent City supporter; naturally I told him we were United fans!

He was really funny; we spent the first half of the night finding as many words to say sick as possible and the second half trying to think of the worse swear words we knew. We took the mickey mirthlessly out of 'Southern softies' and the Marinites. I have not laughed that much in a long, long time.

I couldn't believe it when I later found out that he is a prominent Orthopaedic Surgeon! We have planned to meet up with him at his favourite drinking hole, that bloody Biker bar. Apparently he took his boss there for a business lunch!

Cracking bloke.

July 24th, 2005

OUT THE PARK

We were very lucky this week to have been invited, as clients, to watch a Baseball Game. As you may be aware this is the National Sport and the local team is The San Francisco Giants.

We were in a private box with a nice girl who served us food and wine.

However this did not stop Ben from insisting I walk three miles to the nearest pizza joint with Leo giving a Darth Vader, may the force be with you demonstration to just about anyone who looked at him plus giving all said people high fives!

Now, Baseball here is a huge day out and it appeals to every age group and is very much a family occasion. The stadium the Giants play at is called the SBC stadium and is right on the Bay front, one side of the 'diamond' is completely open to the bay! You can see canoes in the water waiting to catch the balls that are hit 'out the park'. Apparently when their star player, Barry Bonds, plays there are lots of boats out there as he slugs the ball so hard they end up in the bay!

My evaluation of the game was that it was a girlie game of Rounders played by fat geezers on steroids (allegedly...) wearing jodhpurs...the rules being you fielded till you were in and batted till you were out but no-one ran too hard to the bases?!

Not exactly an adrenaline rush but fun all the same. We did laugh as Ben and Sam knew all the songs and all the chants plus all the rules. All this and yet have never been or watched a game in their life! It's a bloody long game though, three hours later we were the only ones still in the box. Everyone else had buggered off home!

One of the Giants team is called Moises Aloo, I couldn't understand why, every time it was his turn to bat the crowd called out "Boo" when he was deffo one of the better players. I asked the fans in the next box why this was and he said they weren't calling out Boo but Alooooo!

Must say I felt a bit of a idiot!

Anyway, it was a fun night, even if the Giants did lose 6-4.

What is interesting is each town is fully behind its own team. You know how at home in England, in one classroom you would have kids supporting Arsenal, Chelsea, Liverpool or any other team? Well here, there is only one town, one team so, at a match there are no visiting team supporters as it is just too far to travel to watch your teams' away games and so the opposing team has no crowd support at all.

On Tuesday it was my turn to host the International Mothers group meeting. Thank-God I'm like me Mam and cater for an army as 20 people turned up! We had a really nice evening and got round to discussing embarrassing moments with famous people.

One of the girls is a drama teacher, the local Garden centre, each summer, puts on an outdoor performance of one of Shakespeares' plays. Now, Sean Penn lives next door to the Garden Centre and one day popped in to see the kids rehearsing. My friend, not realizing who he was shooed him off thinking he was a pervie much to the total mortification of her students!

No-one, it was unanimously agreed, managed to beat mine.

I stayed at the Yale Club in New York to look for a house after Nigel was offered a job on Wall Street. It was the 6 month anniversary of 9/11 and I was on the top floor of the hotel in the restaurant sitting at my sad bastard table for one. Upon hearing my English accent the couple on the table next to me started up a conversation by asking me where I was from.

Now, you know when you know someones' face but can't put a name to it? Well, I spent a pleasant time with this couple talking about how the city was coping following 9/11 and how at bad times people pull together and about what I was doing there. They told me all about a nephew who worked for this same company Nigel had been offered a job with. All the time I am referring to them as mother and son... she looking noticeably granny like and him looking distinctly middle aged. It was only as I was leaving that the waiter told me it was George Bush Senior and his WIFE Barbara. Nige was totally mortified when he found out, I was more than slightly embarrassed myself!

Yesterday we went to another of Queenies' pool parties. Her hubby introduced me to a new drink call Gin Fizz, the rest of the afternoon remains a blur but I am sure a good time was had by all!

Today, after Abbie's Lovey classes we went off to the local park. It is always really busy there with lots going on. There is always a game of Baseball or sand volleyball and the picnic tables are almost all full. There is another game played too called Horseshoes where there is a wooden stump and you have three horseshoes to hook over the stump.

On Sundays there is a team of expats that go to play cricket there. At the end of August they play the 'Ashes'!

For once we don't have much planned for the coming week. It actually felt a bit chilly today.

Only 77 degrees!

The Giants Stadium

August 14th, 2005

COO, EEE WE'RE BACK!

Well, it has been a bit of a manic four weeks, so much so that last night I went to bed at 8:30 pm and slept all the way through to 9am this morning!

My sister and her husband left yesterday, it was lovely to have them but it also made me realize that in the animal kingdom siblings never stay together for life and there's a jolly good reason for that!

Speaking of siblings, Nigels' sister moved to Taiwan on Friday with her two sons. As much as I dislike many of the Marinites that I have met, at least they swear at me in English!

Do not envy the Sister in law at all.

We had our trip away in the Winnebago and had another wonderful time accept for one awful campsite and erm, one rather major crash.

All of the campsites, with one exception, were ones we had stayed at last year. The exception was one that, according to the book, was within walking distance of 7 restaurants and was in the countryside. The reality was it was a truck stop in the desert. The seven restaurants were all attached to garages and were all McDonald and KFC types!

The heat was unbelievable and when I ventured to the dark shower rooms a rat ran across my foot!

We had a fab time; Nigel was not quite so obsessed this time with cleaning the floor of the Winnie.

Since returning my sister informs me that she did not get to see Rocky the raccoon but that we do now have a Skunk who has been named Flowers!

One of my friends has persuaded me to join the school PTA and in my absence signed me up for being next years Car Lot Organiser.

Apparently I will be responsible for organizing a class Rota for opening car doors to speed up the morning and afternoon drop off and pick up!

Sounds like a disaster in the making to me.

August 21st, 2005

HELLO MY LOVELIES

Well, I now feel more or less back to my former self and I realize that I told you hardly anything about our trip in the last newsletter.

Our route was pretty much the same as last year, we just ensured we did all the fabulous things we didn't have time for last year. My brother-in-law, Ian, drove us to Santa Cruz to pick up the Winnie, which is about an hour North of here, and after a night spent there we headed down towards the Mexican border, south of San Diego. We spent a few days in LA visiting all the famous beaches such as Laguna, Venice and Santa Monica. It is really all the same beach, but it just goes for miles along the coast. Laguna Beach is a real 'Artiste' hangout with tons of galleries and is quite 'pozy', my fella Brad lives here with that Angie bint.

Santa Monica, it is really very Hollywoodesk- just walking along the beach 'prom' we stopped to watch filming going on, one was a music video, people here are so blasé about it all that they bitch about the inconvenience of being asked to wait a few minutes while a set is shot!

The kids hired Roller blades and Leo had a very attractive purple bike, complete with tassels on the handle bars, and also sporting a Spiderman helmet!

Lining the sidewalk are hundreds of stalls selling art, books, palm reading and clothes. The sand is pure white and feels like flour underfoot and is spotless but the cafes along the sea front are vile little greasy spoons and the air is thick with smog or, because we are in Hollywood, the 'marine' layer!

In Santa Monica we parked up on the beach and then headed into town for dinner, the pier was off limits due to a huge party for Fox films, we stood watching the paparazzi take pictures of all the Celebes arriving in their Limos'.

We ended up at a cozy restaurant on 3rd Street which is a pedestrian street with all the best restaurants and shops on it. Lining the route were lots of street entertainers, some of which were a bit risqué which did make us cringe a bit with the kids there! It reminded me of the great entertainment to be seen on Eastgate

Street in Chester, my home town. As is the custom here, we had a 'doggie' bag of leftovers after our meal. Whilst Nigel was watching a break dance group perform their moves I gave the remainder of his rack of lamb and chicken breast to a tramp... her need was greater than ours!

We visited Carmel where Clint Eastwood is / was Mayor. It is a really pretty and very affluent town. The beach there is gorgeous and has lots of chipmunks that would eat out of your hand, which amused the kids no end and me less so when one ran off with Leo's shoe and was never seen again...

Our disastrous accident happened in LA on our way back home. Now, at this point I need to point out that our Winnie was more or less brand new – it had only 9,000 on the clock and you could still smell the 'newness' that only comes with new cars or, bizarrely, new dolls. It was, therefore, rather embarrassing phoning the hire company to explain we had just totally trashed their pride and joy! The damage was extensive to say the least, most of the passenger side, from front to back, where Leo and I were sat, was ripped to pieces. I thank my lucky stars that we were OK as we could see what was going to happen seconds before impact. One of the boys was kneeling on the floor between the two front seats, talking to Nigel and I. I just had time to fling my arm across to stop him hurtling between us and through the front window. Poor Abbie was lying asleep, strapped across two seats and was unaware, until impact, to what was happening. All the cupboards flew open and spewed their contents everywhere and the mattresses flew off the beds. I was just so scared that a pile up would occur. The stupid woman that caused the accident by gabbing on her cell phone is lucky she still has all her teeth. Nigel had to hold me back from thumping her one; at no stage whatsoever did she ask if we were unhurt, she never got off that bloody cell phone. Thankfully we had a camera and took loads of pictures for the police.

She has since admitted liability but showed no remorse whatsoever for hitting a van with four kids in, she never asked once if they were hurt.

Biznatch!

A very bizarre thing happened when we got home. At Nigels' Christmas do, last year, as we were leaving the hotel, the entrance was lined with logs on either side; Nigel managed to get the car stuck on one of these logs so that whether we moved backwards or forwards we were jammed! Consequently we ended up dragging the log on the front bumper and undercarriage causing the front bumper to cave in. We have spent the months since arguing about whose responsibility it was to take the car in to be fixed! After returning home it dawned on us that the dent on the car had disappeared totally! It is still the same bumper as the scratch is there but the elephant sized dent has gone!

I called the garage and they said it is not unusual for dents to 'pop' out again in very hot weather! How freaky is that?

This week is the last one of the school holidays and quite frankly the kids are bordering on hideous now, although I do feel a little sorry for Abbie as she has had six hours of maths tutoring each week plus her luvvy classes! So, she does not feel she has had much of a break but she has been very gracious about it all!

I did, however, have to double her pocket money in order to get her to agree to a ton of maths lessons throughout the holidays!

This week marks a week of purgatory for me . . . the start of soccer season! We have literally just had the training schedule and already I am back to training four nights a week with matches all day Saturday!

This week I promised the kids they could each have a pool party so I have been busy inventing non alcoholic cocktails for them!

I am pleased they are going back to school, 12 weeks is a ridiculous length of time to be away from learning.

I am starting to feel very anxious about our return home. I have not managed to find a Return to Nurse Practice Course near our UK house and I am fed up of renting homes to live in, I did say to Nigel that after being married for 12 years the next home we bought I was going to be very reluctant to leave! He did point out that he was surprised I knew how long we have been married as, apparently, I had forgotten our 12 year anniversary.

Oops!

September 5th, 2005

BETTER LATE THAN NOT AT ALL

Well, we have had a truly mad, sometimes funny, occasionally tearful and other times plain daft two weeks!

It has been a case of hit the ground running after 12 weeks of merely lying on it! What a complete shock to the system to be back to getting up at 6am, running round like your feet are on fire and not cooling down until 11pm!

The school day is just SO busy here, I can only try to explain how it is.

Due to the fact that Music lessons are not part of the national curriculum, they are paid for by the school PTA, but only if you live in an affluent area, then in order for your child to participate in music then they must have their lessons in what is known as zero period hours. Basically the child needs to be in school at 7:30am before school officially starts. As Abbie is in the school band then I have to take her to school at 7:30 am twice a week, that's no easy thing with four kids!

Having spent the last two weeks trying to co-ordinate the Car parking Rota for the parents of 590 kids, 33 classes and for 37 weeks I have been taking night time flu medicine to help me sleep!

I maintain what I have always known that I am a sheep and NOT a Shepherd! I have spent every morning and every afternoon showing up at school to open frigging car doors and giving as much abuse as I am receiving and now I am knackered! These parents never cease to amaze me with their total and utter arrogance and rudeness!

As if things were not bad enough, last week-end was a farce, at least I can now see the funny side (just). Nigel was away and, just for once I had managed to sneak into the shower without Leo. Consequently I had the shower really hot and was taking my time. As I was getting out, I could hear running water in the heating ducts. I ran out of my bedroom to find the toilet cistern in the kids' bathroom pumping water across the landing and down into the heating shaft! As an immediate measure I threw down the towel I was wearing across the nearest 'lake' and after grabbing the phone to call the landlord began running around the house in search of the water shut off valve. The landlord informed me it was outside… so there I am stark naked, swearing profusively running around the outside of the house looking for the valve when the mother of Abbies' pal, who had stayed overnight, arrived to pick up her daughter for her 'ballet' lesson! Well, what she saw was about as far removed from Swan Lake as you could ever get!

Life has been one long learning curve this week. Firstly I became aware of just how savvy my two year old is. One day, in the lounge, Leo was happily playing on the floor when I noticed a 'cable' on the couch.

Speaking aloud, as you do, when alone with a two year old, I said,

"Oh, I wonder what this is?"

To which Leo looked up and said,

"Charger, game boy SP."

Scary!

So, as well as school starting so has the dreaded soccer season. I have somehow managed to become the 'team' parent and therefore copped making up a snack roster for all the matches. This would be fine if it were not for wheat, nut, dairy, kosher, vegan and vegetarians to consider as well as the plain mad to cater for!

To make things worse I somehow manage to cop writing a team song! I thought I was an utter clever arse as the team is called 'Lightning' so I just changed the words to Grease Lightening. When it came to present my song for the teams' approval I had printed the words off and said it was to be sung to the tune of, to my horror the coach insisted I sang it. So, other than a Tuesday we are at a soccer practice every night, so now Abbie has been asked to join the cross country running team which trains on a … Tuesday!

My darling baby starts Pre School tomorrow which makes me feel very weepy. When we talk about going, he says

"And mummy"

I will feel lost without him as since we moved here he has been my constant side kick, and, I know I am biased, but he is so much fun to have around and makes me laugh so much!

As I am sure, many of you have already seen the truly devastating results of a hurricane in New Orleans. There are appeals on TV all the time for aid, it is such a sad situation, the whole area seems to be extremely poor.

The majority of houses are built 4 feet below sea level. Thousands of buses were sent out to evacuate people but most people didn't know where to go so just sat tight. All rescue attempts were hindered by the swamps surrounding the area as they overflowed so there were alligators and huge snakes in the streets. So far thousands are believed to have perished. Even Fats Domino is missing.

We have a huge old jar on the kitchen windowsill which moves from house to house with us. We fill it with all the loose change and when it is full the kids choose a charity to donate the money to. Over the last few years, I am proud to say that we have been able to help support many charities, including 9/11, the kings Cross Fund, Tsunami fund and to-day we posted off a cheque for $200 to the Red Cross for the hurricane Katrina Fund. All from a jar that eats loose change that is never missed. We have even adopted a donkey at the Potten End Donkey Sanctuary!

This week-end we have seen many lemonade and cookie stands in aid of a chosen charity, obviously they are all donating to the Katrina fund at present. I think this is a fab way for kids to help their communities, and it's amazing how much more money is raised when it is kids asking for the money! A friend to-day raised $300 in an HOUR for the Katrina fund! Just to let the halo slip a moment, on Friday night we went to a party held in a friends' garden. It is held every year and is hosted by four families to welcome all new families to the school.

Well, one of the families that host this is an English / American couple.

He is terribly English and went to Cambridge (flogs houses for a living).

His family in the UK is from Henley on Thames, his wife works for a museum in San Fran and she affects more of a British accent than he does and she's the American half!

Anyway, by the end of the night they were arguing as to whom to invite for an upcoming dinner party, those from the British Consulate or those from the British Embassy!

Decision, decisions...

When I suggested they ask Liz, Phil and the Corgi's be invited too Nigel decided it was time to go home . . . the spoilsport.

Something else that made me laugh this week. When we were away in the Winnie my sister and her husband met a 'casting' agent by the name of Randy who eventually contacted me because they just 'adored' Abbie.

They are probably very professional but could you really send your 12 year old daughter to appear in a Randy Film Production?

I think not.

September 11th, 2005

SKUNKTASIA

Our house smells, really, really smells . . . so badly that when you walk in the front door your eyes sting and you gag.

It would seem that Flowers the skunk has moved in under the house to have her babies and is spraying her nest, liberally. We assume she has abandoned her last abode due to the fact that our landlords have workmen in removing the fence along the drive and replacing it with a retaining wall, complete, I must add, with a set of stone steps for the deer!

Deer are creatures of habit and always follow the same route; we have a visible trail through the wilderness around the house. The fence along the drive took a regular beating as the deer would jump the fence into the wilderness; the steps are to provide easier access!

We have been advised that the only way to get rid of Flowers is to shine a constant bright light into her nest and drip ammonia into it. I feel this is a tad drastic so we have decided to just be very anti-social for a few weeks and hope she has her babies and then buggers off. I quite like the idea of having a house that smells so bad at the week-ends that no one wants to sleep over!

Nigel is away again, I did tell him on the phone that for the inconvenience caused by him being absent for the first two weeks back at school that he had better come home with something small, sparkly and is weighed in carats. This is opposed to something red, nylon and lacy wrapped in tissue paper. . . I swear I could hear him rustling for the receipt!

Leos' first week at school was rather traumatic for us both. On the first day I stayed for 20 minutes to get him settled and then told him I was going off to do some jobs and then I'd be back for him. He seemed quite happy and went off without a backward glance. However, when I went back to get him, he burst into tears and the staff told me he had sat by the door with his dummy and his 'Snugger' all day without eating or letting them change his nappy.

God, my heart broke! It must have seemed like forever to him. When we got home we had a little talk and he said

"Me no like man, he no change my bum."

So, the next day he seemed quite happy to go back again. I quietly asked his teacher if it was possible for one of the lady teachers to change Leos' 'diaper' as he had been very upset about the man doing it. She looked at me for a moment and then told me that, actually, there were no male teachers at the school . . .

I have also had to explain all the English terminology to the staff so that they will understand what Leo wants. For example diaper is nappy and dummy is a pacifier, words that we take for granted that anyone working with children would know. It is surprising just how many different words we use, another example is we would say pushchair or pram but here both are called a stroller.

On Saturday morning we were all up and out at 9am for our 1st soccer match in hippie town Fairfax. I was first on the snack rota so I arrived with a huge cooler box, on wheels, full of drinks, mini bagels and mini pots of Philadelphia cheese! It was a hard match, Abbie scored two goals and they drew two all. Ruby and I stood on the sidelines singing Go Team Lightning to the Grease tune and had a great little dance move to go with it. Every time our team had the ball we would sing louder. God, the look of utter disgust on our daughters' faces was priceless!

After that game it was home for lunch, plus pal, and then repacking the cool box and onto the second match of the day for Sam and Bens' team. I have this soccer mum thing down to an art form now. I even bought a mini marquee from Costco that I pop up on the sidelines for the team to sit under at half time. Complete, I must add, with old cleaning bottles with a spray function to cool the players down with water when they come off the pitch!

If you think I am bad, one of the other mums on Abbies' team has bought them all a hand towel and stitched their names onto them, AND she takes them home each week to wash and brings them to the next game in a cool box!

Following a three goal draw it was off to Safeway for some BBQ grub and onto a great party in a park hosted by the International Mothers Group. It was a lovely few hours, it is amazing how much you appreciate being with other Brits who understand your terminology and sense of humour. Nigel and I had been planning on having a 'Trailer Trash' party where everyone comes dressed in faux

Leopard skin and white stilettos and eats Spam Fritters. We have now changed our minds and decided on having an International party where everyone comes dressed in their traditional costume and brings a plate of their country's native food. In my case then that's a Leopard skin dress and white stilettos. .

Tonight was a time of reflection. The Dad of one of Abbies' friends called me and said that his daughter, as part of her homework, had to choose a famous speech to read out to the class and explain its importance, meaning and impact. As a Dad he had recommended to her the infamous speech by Sir Winston Churchill. He put his phone on loud speaker and asked me to talk to her about what that speech might have meant to the British Nation at that time. I did so, to the best of my ability, which was crap to be honest.

It got me thinking, so I asked my own kids what, if anything, they knew about Winston Churchill or the Second World War. Abbie vaguely remembered studying it in Year 4 in Primary school but of course the boys were here in Year 4 so they had no clue at all who he was.

This Dad of Abbies' friend had assumed that as a child both myself and my kids had been educated on this speech and of its significance and historical place in English history.

It made me realize that maybe, we take our history for granted, for whatever reason, but that here history is still being 'made'. All children at the local schools can recite at least part of Martin Luther Kings' speech "I have a dream" and have some understanding of what that message was. They are expected to learn speeches off by heart and examine the meaning and implications.

It just made me think just how many English children, when asked, would even know who Churchill was?

Ask your kids and find out.

This coming week does not hold anything exciting, the most interesting thing I plan on doing is checking my mileage just to see how many miles I really do with all the to-ing and fro-ing each week.

Oh, whilst I remember, god, have been here too long, we have a mountain lion on the prowl. When the weather gets hot as it is now they come further and further down the mountain in search of food and water.

Everyone irrigates their gardens to keep the grass lush and so the lions come down. Residents are being advised NOT to be alone after dusk and not to leave pets in the garden unattended! In the local paper this week it showed a photo of a lion dragging a deer out of someones garden very close to us!

Anyone seen Raffy Roo . . . ?

September 18th, 2005

FROM THE ENGLISH BIRD IN MARIN

It is that time again, the boys are grooving to Greenday in the basement with pals, Abbie, looking very glam, is engrossed in a documentary on the Vietnam War, Leo is running around in his Halloween outfit and Nigel is snoring out by the pool!

Me, I am shut in the computer room with the shades down, the door locked and a bottle of Rioja to my right!

The madness continues, somehow when I planned the car duty rota for school I managed to put Sam and Bens' classes first so I have to do car duty yet again, for two weeks running! Some people never cease to amaze me, on Thursday; after the second bell had already rung there was the usual mad rush of cars. Some daft bint stopped her car in the middle of the line and took 6 minutes and 15 seconds (I counted...) to say Goodbye to her kids. Then she casually starts moving the car seat to a different place! There were 21 cars blocked behind her which, by now, were backing onto the main road and causing chaos at the traffic lights!

I could hold my temper no longer and shouted across to her to move NOW! Well, I got the middle finger, abuse from the car window, several cars behind her started and all hell let loose. I just stood there with my cuppa tea and laughed! When I had to go into the office to hand my 'uniform' in I told the staff I was not going out there again unless they provided me with a Baseball bat!

The parents are just dreadful, I think they feel incredibly pressured if the kids are late because then it gets taken out on the kids. They have to report to the office and get a 'tardy' pass which then makes them feel bad and humiliated for the rest of the day.

On Monday I went for my first Parent / Teacher Association (PTA) meeting, the only reason being that Jenn is the head of it this year and so I went to morally support her as it was her first meeting. It was fascinating; it was all very professional and formal. There were about 60 people there in total. All together they raise $1.1 MILLION a year! This covers art, computer and music classes which are NOT part of the National Curriculum and so if you want your kids to have access to these then the parents have to raise the funds themselves.

Make you feel lucky?

The PTA also finances extra teachers / teaching assistants to help keep classes down to 20. It also pays for fresh fruit, bottled water and newspapers in the Staff room of both the Primary and Middle school. Teachers here earn a basic salary of $65,000 and get very well looked after in this particular district.

One of the fundraising initiatives is the 'Parent Giving Campaign' that runs each October. They ask that each family 'give' $825 per child, so, for us that's $2,575 a year for a state school, not including school outings or lunches or equipment.

Last year, in the school information book they printed the names of all the families and how much money each of them had given! Not only that, but the names were put into groups for everyone to see!

Pikeys – for those who gave under $825
Hikers – for those that gave $825
Mountaineers – for those that gave over $825!

Friends here laugh when I tell them that at the PTA in England we were really proud of ourselves to raise £40,000 to buy a new climbing frame for the kids, and that our PTA meetings were held in the pub or at someones house over a bottle of wine and a bag of nuts!

On Tuesdays I have volunteered to be the school 'dinner bag'. In Primary school to me this meant Mrs. Johnson who pulled out all my baby teeth with cotton! Just as proof that your sins will come back to haunt you, when Nigel and I got married Mrs. Johnson was then the Church Warden and was the one rearranging my dress and veil in the vestry with a vengeance!

It was an OK experience (being the dinner bag!); the kids here have lots to do at break time. I have had to learn all the rules for games I have never heard of! All of the other dinner bags have a whistle to control the kids. Personally I prefer to use plain old fear! The kids are really lucky actually as there is a PE teaching assistant, a French guy, who spends his entire break and lunch time out on the field playing team sports with the kids. They just love him, he makes me laugh too, he's very French and not very conventional at all!

Last week when we went to bed (Nige and I, not the French guy...) we could hear a party going on next door, fine, no problem, until we hear an argument where death threats are being made and it occurs to us that the parents are away. Things began to get nasty and the argument spilled out onto the street. It is really weird because we could hear all this because we live in a canyon but cannot see the neighbours' house! We lasted until 1 am listening to some poor guy trying to mediate an escalating bad, bad situation, by this time our kids have woken up too and we gave in and called the police to report a 'disturbance'. Much to our horror not only did the police turn up but the bloody Fire Brigade! I was mortified thinking that a lone police Cruiser would arrive, quietly diffuse the situation and then bugger off. Alas not, apparently the Fire Brigade always come out as they are medically trained and more often than not will arrive before an ambulance.

Hope I don't run into the neighbours' for a while!

I did have a laugh this week, because Leo has started pre-school he had to have an 'assessment' at the Doctors. Now here, they don't have Health Visitors so you see the Doctor for all general health checkups.

Now, our Pediatrician is the most miserable South African bastard you will ever meet. He has zero bedside manner and, quite frankly, I don't think he even likes children. At Leo's check up he told me that he thought it was time that 'Percy was shown the porcelain'. This is a man who tried to convince me that Leo had some serious neurological disorder and should be seen by a host of Specialists, because he did not walk but shuffled on his bottom, as I had done as a baby.

I told him that the only job I thought he would be crapper at was being a Gynaecologist, he told me the only woman he thought was tougher than me was his wife. The guy is a total moron!

Sam bribed me to-day to do a lemonade stand to help raise money for the Hurricane Katrina Fund, by doing so they added another $95 to what they have sent already. What a star!

I did something very American this week, I went to see a chick flick on my own, very liberating!

For my book club this week we have just finished 'The Song Lines' by Bruce Chatwin and we are now reading 'the English Patient'. I always find it difficult to read the book after seeing the movie...

Until next time.

September 25th, 2005

I CAN BREATHE CLEARLY NOW THE SMELL HAS GONE AND ALL OBSTACLES ARE OUT MY WAY.

Flowers has left the building ...... thank f**k for that!

The builders have left for a Spanish holiday (Magaluff?) and Flowers has fled and will hopefully not return!

It has been a relatively quiet week in the Barrett household for a change!

Abbie and Leo have been off school with really horrid colds and ear infections; I think these are the first illnesses we have had in a year, so that's not bad at all.

This has not, however, stopped me writing a snotty letter to Abbies' teacher! All of my kids had ONE day off school last year following a long weekend of feeling poorly. This does not stop the school from sending out rude letters stipulating how much funding the school has lost each time your child is off sick. Whilst I fully appreciate this is done, in part, for those who keep their kids home for no good reason it really pissed me off that I got a letter for one frigging day! Not only that but for every day a kid is off school here they expect the child to make up ALL lessons they missed while ill and, in their own time, and, on top of a heavy homework schedule. Consequently I feel they were off sick due to being 'run down' and now poor Abbie is so fraught trying to catch up with what she missed I worry she will make herself ill again!

Other than that life is quite calm, nothing new. The weather is perfect and Saturday was the usual bedlam of soccer matches. This week was very flattering for the boys as an article ran in the local paper about Sam and Ben saying they were the "two toughest players to appear in the local soccer league in a long time", which was nice for them to read.

On Saturday night I went to the cinema with two girls, one, Jenn, is a good friend and the other has twin boys who are pals of Sam and Ben.

She is a housewife now but B.K (before kids) she was a pilot flying fighter jets for the US army. How cool is that?!

We went to see The Constant Gardener which I thought was a fabulous film, not what I expected at all.

To-day, after Abbies 'lovey' classes we went for a hike around Lake Laginitas which is one of our favourite places. A sure sign that Leo is growing up is that he managed to walk most of the 2 miles around the lake. It is such a calm, tranquil place to be. The scenery is stunning, there is an enormous lake, amazing birds, giant redwood trees and, at this time of year hundreds of turtles sunning themselves on logs in the lake.

The back drop is rolling hills and pastures and yet all this is walking distance from the town (village to us) of Ross. It is just a lovely place to spend a Sunday afternoon with the family and the dog.

Nothing much planned for the rest of the week, just the usual organized mayhem! There is so much more to do here, the pace of life is so much faster it is hard to put the brakes on and put things in perspective and not get utterly swept up in the madness of it all. Sometimes I want to take a deep breath and shout 'STOP', everyone just relax!

So, we have got through an entire week with no disasters or drama which feels rather odd! So, this is what a normal family feels like?!

Nigel is trying to convince me that he NEEDS a motorbike. I told him I NEED a weekend in Las Vegas at the Casinos and NEED $30,000 to spend whilst I am there with the 5 mates I'm treating . . .

He's skulked off to rethink his ideas . .

October 3rd, 2005

TEXT BOOK CASE

When checking my E mails this week I received one from eBay, congratulating me on my winning a bid for . . . a Ducati ST3 2004!

It can only be considered as a text book case of a man about to hit a 40 type thing to do!

Apparently my darling hubby has bought this bike from a place in Philadelphia which is probably nearer to you! When I asked him how he was planning on getting it here he suggested that he and I fly out there and, get this, we ride it the 6,000 miles back . . . shall not repeat what my own suggestion to that was.

I did ask if this meant that the Audi 2 seater sports car would be going but, apparently not. Now, I would like to point out that Nige has never actually been on a motorbike in his life but is promising to take Abbie to school on it. . over my dead body was the reply to that one.

I am a little narked off to say the least!

This week has gone very fast, the weather has been in the 90's so I have been out walking a lot when Leo is at nursery; to-day was the first day with no tears when I left him. Bless him.

On Thursday and Friday I had sodding Car Duty again BUT that's my turn over until February.

On Friday afternoon our Landlady came over with her daughter and we spent the afternoon having some really interesting discussions about the differences between our two countries. The daughter has the same opinion as me about why the Americans are so puritanical, Californians in particular. That is, that the first settlers to arrive in San Francisco, about 1849, were Puritans who arrived here to help 'save' the souls of all those people who raced here for the Gold Rush. As a result many of them stayed and established Missions so, what we now have are all their descendants.

Makes sense to me anyhow!

I was very excited on Saturday, as some of you may know I was a huge fan of the rock band Journey back in the 80's. Well, I found out that they live in Novato, about 15 minutes North of here, and they were performing at a fund raising concert for their kids' schools. So, I was all set to get up there but then found out they were not appearing until 6pm and we had plans to go out.

Bummer!

Abbie has since informed me that her pal that lives at the back of us is the God daughter of one of the band members and gets up on stage to sing with them. It is such a coincidence to live so near them, none of my friends in England had even heard about them when I was a teenager.

On Sunday we were invited to a jazz concert in a place called Nicasio which is about ½ an hour west of here. It is a beautiful drive through hills the colour of straw. All we saw for miles were horse ranches, and the actual centre of Nicassio reminded me of the tiny town in Little House on The Prairie. There is a paddock in the middle surrounded by white clapboard houses and a barn and church with a red pitched roof. There is a long low building that houses the general store, post office and the saloon. At the back of the saloon was this green oasis overlooking hills dotted with grazing horses. There was a BBQ set up and everyone took a blanket or deckchair and plonked themselves down in a space, there was a beer tent and the bands played in the shade of an awning. It all felt quite surreal, apparently they have bands every week and if the weather is too cold they move indoors. It was a very pleasant afternoon, good music, great BBQ and beautiful surroundings and all in lovely sunshine!

Throughout October there is a Pumpkin Patch where you come to pick your own pumpkin for Halloween as well as mazes for the kids to get lost in. Sounds a whole lot more fun than choosing one in the fruit and veg aisle in Tesco's!

Next week is the annual Pancake Breakfast fundraiser at the local fire station where the firemen cook the breakfasts and the kids get to sit in the engines and play with the hoses. Naturally this means I have the total hair and beauty works and might even shave my legs and try not to drool over the gorgeous, yummy, hunky, sexy men in their uniforms . . . obviously we go just for the kids' enjoyment and to support our local Fire Station and to act like good citizens of the community..

That same night we are off to school for a spaghetti dinner and talent show. This is a fun fund raiser where a local company provides all different types of pasta and salad and the tables are all set up outside in the playground with red check tablecloths and the kids 'wait' on the parents. After all the food everyone piles into the sports hall and the kids put on a talent show, some of them are great!

Coming up soon is the good old 'Parent Giving' campaign. No doubt I shall be up in arms over the latest ridiculous gimmicks they want us to participate in, I wonder how deep we will be asked to dig into our pockets this time round?

For now I am off to check on Nige's life insurance policy.

Nigel on the 'Death Machine'.

The Queen Mary entering the Bay under the Golden Gate Bridge.

October 20th, 2005

JUST CALL ME MILLIE

It's been a hectic couple of weeks, no change there then! The weather is still very hot in the afternoons but the fog rolls in each morning. It really is bizarre, we have the heating on in the mornings and yet send the kids to school in shorts and tee shirts, smothered in factor 30 plus a jumper!

It is prime fire season at the moment as it has been months since it last rained, there is a widespread ban on BBQ's and the sound of the fire engines racing up the mountain is an almost everyday occurrence. There are lots of deer, snakes, raccoons and the odd lion about as they come down from the mountain to the residential areas in search of water to be found in the irrigated gardens. In Southern California, such as Los Angeles and San Diego, there is no natural water supply and so it is pumped from the North of the state some 400 miles down!

It is strange to think that there are huge deserts, the Mojave desert for example, that take hours to cross right here in California.

As for the snakes, I nearly freaked out totally when walking with Raffy recently. We met up for a hike with a friend and her dog. While we were walking along the dogs were off in the bush when her dog was bitten by a rattlesnake! I was under the impression that they were not indigenous to this area as it is not generally hot enough for them. Since then I have heard from another friend that her neigbour had one in her garage!

The wildlife here still freaks me out at times. One of Nigel's colleagues has a second home up at Lake Tahoe where the ski resorts are. He and his family went up a few weeks ago to find that a bear had broken the window to the garage, opened the connecting door to the kitchen, raided the fridge and then had crapped on the kitchen floor!

Imagine waking in the night and coming downstairs for a drink of water and finding a 350lbs Teddy in your kitchen munching your leftovers!!

We have had a couple of cracking nights out lately. The school held a Spaghetti Dinner and talent show. All the tables were set up in the playground and the kids served the adults food and soft drinks. When everyone had finished we all carried our chairs in to the hall for the talent show. It was really, really good! Some kids sang, some danced, and a couple did a sketch from Monty Python- The Life of Bryan. Lovely day for a crucifixion gets you out in the open air, crucifixion party to the left please . . .

Some kids played instruments and sang songs they had written themselves. Considering they were all 14 years and under they were very talented. What struck me is how much more assertive and confident children here are. This is probably down to the public speaking they are expected to do on a regular basis as part of the school curriculum. Our three frequently have to write reports or poetry and present them orally to the whole class.

Last Saturday we went to a friends 40th birthday that was being held at their home. In the open plan living area their furniture had been replaced with tables for two or four people. There were caterers serving sushi and wine, and the entertainment for the evening was two celebrity comedians!

I tell you, these Californians know how to throw a good party! I feel a bit nervous now as we are having a party soon for my International group here at the house.

This is the ultimate party house though; even one of our friends has asked if she can hold her 40th here next year! Apparently she will be having a casino theme and will have Black Jack tables, caterers, Henna tattoo artists and Valet parking on our drive! Are they really that shite at parking their own cars?

I had a funny / bizarre moment recently. It has always concerned me how easy it is to walk onto school grounds unchallenged. Schools are much more part of the community, what we would call the school hall is open to the public to host their own thing. The schools are spread out and have many entrance points.

I made a comment to our landlady about how it made me very nervous whenever I drove past a certain local school and always saw men sitting on park benches and watching the children playing outside on the school field and seemingly unchallenged by staff. Well, she laughed and said that the kids at that school were the last ones I need worry about. The men are all the body guards for the celebrity kids like Sean Penns'!

Ahh, silly me, why didn't I think of that...

You do, however, seem to see a lot of nutters in the community. I was chatting to Sam and Bens P.E. teacher, the French guy, and he had the opinion that this was because the local mentally ill community often do not have medical insurance and cannot therefore afford the drugs they need to control their conditions. Couple this with the fact that when good ole Ronnie Reagan was Governor of California he, allegedly, passed a bill stating that it was an infringement on human rights to force these people to take their medication.

Young adults with severe physical disabilities are also a common sight, particularly amongst the Hispanic population. Again, without medical insurance the majority cannot afford the physiotherapy and rehabilitation needed after suffering things like a stroke. It really makes me appreciate how fortunate we are to have the National Health Service.

It astounds me the vast range and effects of wealth here. At one end of the spectrum there are the multi millionaires living in the mansions and yet in the same community there will be those living in utter poverty in little more that tin shacks like in some third world nation. The Americans are fascinated by what they perceive is our Social class system and yet it is no different here. There are the Haves and the Have Nots and very little in between. If you are successful here then you can have an amazing lifestyle and live the 'American Dream', but for the regular Joe Bloggs life is anything but easy and living conditions far worse than anything I have ever seen in even the roughest, poorest areas of Liverpool.

So, time has been racing away and we have had a great couple of weeks. On Sunday we went off to Stinson Beach with all the kids plus dog and pals. It was wonderful to walk along in the surf wearing shorts and tee shirts in the middle of October! However, we had a reality check to-day when we heard on the local news that a 20 year old girl out surfing had been attacked by a Great White Shark and had survived by punching it on the nose!

As for calling me Miss Millie, well that would be Miss MilliTANT! Yes, I have had yet another run in with the anally exclusive school my darling boys attend. . They must bloody hate me there.

Last week when I picked them up poor Sam burst into tears as soon as he got in the car. When I asked why he said he had got a 'self management card'. Now, you only get one of these for really bad behaviour, get 10 and you are expelled.

Sam got one for . . . running in the library. Apparently, and this is what the teacher wrote on the card she sent us (expecting us to agree wholeheartedly and counter sign it) that Sam had got 'over excited' about a new Star Wars book and had run across the library to show his friend.

Did he hurt someone I asked?

Was he rude to a teacher? I asked

Was he climbing the book shelves? I asked

No, was the answer.

Well, in that case, don't waste my time on stupid bloody trivia came my reply and no, we were not going to sign the ridiculous card.

They are all mad, stark raving bonkers! I would love to put them in an inner city school in London or Liverpool and meet some kids that really do have some serious problems!

On a lighter note, the book in question has been fantastic and has turned Sam into the next Jaime Oliver; ok not quite but it was a bloody recipe book! To-day he brought home the second edition.

Last night he cooked dinner AND made 'Anakin Apple Crisp' dessert.

Tonight Abbie wanted a turn and made 'Darth dogs' and 'Boosk Brownies'!

Punishing a child for showing excitement over a book, what the fook do we send them to school for if not to be excited about learning?

Nutters.

October 30th, 2005

HAPPY HALLOWEEN

Not a very original title but there you go! I cannot believe it is this time of year again! The kids are so very excited as tomorrow they get to go to school in full costume and then, after lunch they have a parade led by the Fire Brigade around the streets surrounding the school and then it's a party in the classrooms where parents are invited and someone reads a scary book and the kids recite spooky poems! Even Leo has a little parade at his school. After that it's out tomorrow night and it really is simply an amazing experience here and ALL the houses join in and some do their houses or garages up as haunted caves that the kids are allowed to walk through! Some houses have strobe lighting and sound effects and there are literally hundreds of kids on the streets. It can get quite stressful trying to find your own little witch and wizards amongst the other 300.

Last week-end we went to the dreaded school fund raiser. We were only going for two hours to show our faces and the invitation said it was very casual. So I wore black trousers and a white tee shirt.

As we walked up the drive to this house where the event was being held imagine how mortified I was to see at least 200 people in Cocktail dresses standing on the lawn of a stunning Hacienda with waitresses and waiters serving 'Cosmos' cocktails from a bar set up around a water fountain!

After a few drinks and hellos we were led through several archways into the 'back' yard where there was an enormous pool with straw cabanas and tall palm trees all around.

It was a full sit down 'do' with hot food and gallons of nice wine. This house was something out of Hello Magazine, just stunning. It was built in the Spanish style forming a U shape around the pool. It was painted terracotta and had curved roof tiles and upstairs balconies with grapevines growing over them.

I did want to giggle though at two huge palm trees that had fairy lights curled up around them.

The desire to yell

"Viva Las Vegas" whilst grinding my hips in an Elvis type way was almost overwhelming!

We were sitting at a table for eight with some really nice people.

Interestingly, none of them are originally from Marin! Once we all got talking, we discovered that all of us had a set of twins, coincidence or what!

So, despite wearing the entirely wrong outfit and having to watch a very cheesy video on how the money we parents give to the school is spent we actually had a very enjoyable evening. It obviously had the desired effect as we then felt obliged to hand over a fat cheque!

This week we have actually had some real rain! I do wish it had come a little sooner as Leo and I went out to water my pots, when I turned on the hose water began spurting out all along the hose tube. The poor Raccoon had obviously bitten through it in desperation to get something to drink!

I must make a point of putting fresh water out for him or I shall be buying a new hose each week!

December 13th, 2005

FROM MINE TO YOURS WITH LOVE

This is the last of my newsletters for 2005, it seems hard to believe that this is the second calendar Christmas we have been here, and how different it is!

Nigel showed me an article this week saying that Tony Blair feels the UK should be more politically correct like the Americans, and instead of us saying Happy Christmas we should say 'Happy Holiday' so as not to offend other religions. I really do hope the British Public does not allow this to happen as it makes for no fun at all. It is almost clandestine the way a few people here put up decorations and fight for the right to say Happy Christmas rather than Happy Holiday. Although a few houses are done up like Blackpool Illuminations, it is very difficult to find a Christmas card that actually says Happy Christmas anywhere on it. I find this so very sad, I am not offended by other religions and I would certainly not expect others to change their traditions and customs so as not to offend my beliefs or culture. If I were to go on holiday in Saudi Arabia, I would respect their culture, not expect them to change it because I was there. This is PC gone barmy. We will end up with a world with no traditions or culture and people too afraid to believe in anything for fear of reprisals.

On Thursday night there is a 'winter song concert' at Sam and Bens' school (no Christmas carols allowed). Where's the festive spirit in that?

Ben has decided that he wants to wear a Tuxedo, bless him. So, tomorrow we are off to have one altered, and he picked out a red dickey bow and matching Cummerbund. He says he will look dashing!

Over the week-end Nigel and I went off to Petaluma (45 minutes drive north East) for his intensive motorbike course, at the end of which he had his test and unfortunately he passed!

On Saturday night we went off to the beach to a house being rented by a colleague of Nigels so as to host his 40th birthday. The road to Stinson Beach is enough to make a naval captain with 30 years experience want to barf. It is like a corkscrew for 9 miles with a sheer drop on one side in places.

Add thick fog to that and it really is not a pleasant drive and even worse at night. The only good bit was seeing all the deer and raccoons, I would have liked to have seen some lions hunting but alas not.

The house, when we eventually found it, was fab and right on the beach, literally. It was really spacious and slept 12 with a huge open plan living area with an enormous fire to roast marshmallows on. Perfect.

Speaking of wildlife, on the way to school this morning there was a dead skunk on the road, hopefully not Flowers, and the smell was just horrific and that was from inside the car! Even after the carcasses disappear the smell of skunk lasts for days. Once you have smelt a skunk, you can recognize the smell forever. It really makes your eyes water! It's like stale pee and really horrendous body odour!

This week was also book club which I always really enjoy. We meet the first Monday of every month in a café in San Rafael. We all have a glass or two of wine and get dinner cheaply too. It has huge sofas and chairs and lots of different groups meet there. We see actors rehearsing parts or people chatting about a movie they have just seen next door. This last book we have read was the most fascinating and engrossing book I have read in a long time. It's called 'The Other Boleyn Girl' by Phillip Gregory. Like the Da Vinci Code did, it expertly blends both fact and fantasy and is a fabulous read.

Hillbilly house has been playing at Animal Hospital again. We found a huge lizard outside the back door one night when they are usually safely in the cracks of the garden walls. It hissed at us as we went near it. I thought it was just cold so Ben picked it up and put it in a shoe box with rocks and sawdust on top of a hot water bottle! After 48 hours it had perked up so we released it in the garden wilderness. A few days later I was looking out of the kitchen window and saw a little mouse on the path and a hawk hovering overhead. I went out and gave it a little prod to see if it was alive, it gave an awful squeal and rolled over. I would have left it but the hawk was getting closer and anticipating a hot fast food dinner so, I scooped it up and put it in the now vacant shoe box.

After three days intensive care in the warmth and eating hamster food it seemed healthy and lively. It then had the bad manners to snuff it on the day of release!

On Thursday we have my Mum and her partner arriving for their first visit to America to spend Christmas with us. We are really looking forward to seeing them; I have not seen them since February and the kids not for a year. Too long.

We have 15 for Christmas day, a friend of ours moved here from the UK when she was nine and her parents really miss a proper 'traditional' Christmas dinner so she asked if they could join us. The more the merrier I say!

We have been watching on the Yahoo news about the awful explosion at the Buncefield Depot in HemelHempsted, it seems amazing that no-one was killed. Thank goodness it was so early in the morning. The pictures taken from space were spectacular.

The main news here was the execution of 'Tookie' Williams at San Quentin jail which we can see from our kitchen window!

I have been writing this newsletter for almost two years now. In some ways the time has gone so very fast. I thank all of you that have taken the time to drop a line, I greatly appreciate it. There have been many low moments when news from home has really lifted my spirits.

On that note I say from my family to yours I wish you all the happiest of Christmases and a very prosperous New Year.

Ben with poorly gecko.

LIVING WITH THE BUNNIES
A BRITISH FAMILYS' EXILE TO MARIN COUNTY.

YEAR THREE

Contents

January 2nd, 2006

HELLO AND HAPPY NEW YEAR FROM SUNNY CALIFORNIA ...NOT!

Happy 2006 to you all and I hope you had a good un! I have been reading and watching your news and weather and cannot believe how cold it has been. Let me tell you though, I would much prefer the cold to the torrential rain and floods and mudslides that we are experiencing here! We are now on day 15 of almost continual rain and the flooding is awful. We have had hours of power cuts and have struggled to get off the mountain because of the fallen trees and mud on the roads. Some families have lost everything, poor buggers. I am involved in a volunteer drive to give help where we can but imagine what it must be like to lose all your photos of family and special occasions. .

We are grateful we live high up but with the kids being off I have cabin fever big time! There is so little to do locally when the weather is crap, there are no pay as you go leisure centres or museums to visit.

Mum and Harry were over for Christmas which was lovely, we tried a few days sight seeing but I had to keep saying

"If it wasn't for the rain you would be able to see Alcatraz, if it wasn't for the rain you could see the Golden Gate bridge etc!!"

I felt so bad for them coming all this way for continuous rain, apparently this is the worst weather since 1967... Funny how that's the year I was born and how I seem to have a 'gift' for rain. I should move to Africa where they would really appreciate my ability to cause rain, I could make a fortune!

So, for Christmas dinner we had 15 people and had a right proper knees up, all that was missing was the Queens Speech and me Mam made up for that! We played lots of games and Harry and my friends Dad got on really well and hogged the Karaoke all day!

On Christmas morning Nigel fulfilled his promise and in the sheeting rain dived in the pool!! Mum recorded it all, he had said he was going to do it naked but I didn't want the turkey spoiled. Mind you it was that cold his looked like the Turkey...

His latest 'I'm going to be 40 soon' craze is Skydiving … freefall. I'll say no more but what the fook is it with men eh?

We took mum and Harry to a party of some people we met at the beach party we went to a while ago. It was great fun but she nearly killed me when I introduced Harry as her toy boy! Well, what else do you call your mums 76 year old boyfriend?

We had a few good nights out with them which were really lovely. She couldn't believe how much the kids have grown. She is a jammy bugger as well, both on the flight coming over and on their return flight they got upgraded to business class!

New Years Eve was relatively quiet, we went to a friend's house for dinner with the kids and then some other friends had an 'Open House' party from 11am to 8pm where you just called in when you wanted for a drink and a chat. We spent News Day watching the celebrations in London on the computer and teaching the kids how to play poker!

A couple of days before Christmas I thought poor Raffy had developed a tumour on his nose as he suddenly had this disgusting brown growth sticking out. I phoned the vet to rush him down only for a friend to tell me it was a deer tic and using my eyebrow tweezers he pulled it out. That was really friggin' vile!!

And so, tomorrow the kids are back in school although Abbie isn't because 15 of her classrooms are flooded so she is a happy bunny and the boys are truly miffed as, so far, their school is safe to return to.

So as not to commit infacide we joined a 'health club' this week so we had somewhere to take the kids to when it rained. I intend to use it and abuse it as soon as school starts back. Some of the members looked a bit pompous so they better keep out my way or 'Millie' will be back!

We have made the decision to stay another year to improve Nigel's CV so it does look like he can stay in a job longer than 2 years before leaving! I have mixed feelings about our decision, there are still lots of places to see and it will be nice to spend more time with the good friends we have made but it's not home...

This also means we have to move again as the owners of this house want to remodel it and move in themselves. That presents a problem to us because it took us so long to find somewhere and now we have the added issue that we have to find a house within the school district. Here, if you move out of the catchment area then your kids have to leave the school. I dread the thought of moving again, we have done it so many times now that I am sick to death of doing it.

We sat yesterday and planned our year to fit in everything we want to do and see while we have time.

Keep me up to date with what's happening in the real world!

January 16th, 2006

HAPPY MARTIN LUTHER KING DAY

Hello! We are having a long week end as today is Martin Luther King Day.

Had he still been alive he would be 77 years old. He achieved amazing things in his fight for racial equality but it still has a long way to go here. I was talking to some people who had recently been to the deep 'South' and they said that there are still signs outside some restaurants and bars saying 'Whites' only . . . can you imagine that in England? Apparently, visiting places like Alabama are a total shock to the system as the State has not 'progressed' very much at all. California is known as the most progressive State and yet I find it to be very archaic in some ways. You just don't expect America, the so called Super power to be so…backwards in its politics.

Anyway, we have had another busy two weeks since I last wrote. The indoor soccer season is in full swing, both Abbie and the boys' teams remain undefeated thus far. Nige informs me that when he goes to Japan next month I am to coach the team! I tried to explain that these matches are purely a social thing to me and that by the end of the game I generally have no idea what the score is let alone who plays what position!

Last Friday was Nitty Nora the Nit Explorer day, do you remember when we were kids and we all had to line up outside the sick bay while she rummaged through your hair? Well, here it is the parent volunteers that do the rummaging and there is a HUGE stigma about nits it is unbelievable, I was one of the volunteers, we had to stand outside the classrooms with a box of gloves and a box of straws (to part the hair). You should have seen the faces of the other parents when I said that we had all had nits more than once and it was no big deal! Here the kids are sent home if they have them and are treated like Lepers.

This week was also bookclub week. We have just finished reading 'The Queens Fool', by Phillipa Gregory which is a fab book. Our next one is a biography of Lucrezia Borgia. Some of these books are as thick as the bloomin' Bible and I have no time to read anything else!

Nigel and I went out at the weekend and saw a wonderful English / Irish film called Tristan and Isolde, if you get the chance do go and see it, I cried my eyes out at the end! We saw it in our local 'movie' theatre which has only one screen and shows 'select' films which may or may not make it onto the average screen. It was reopened two years ago after being closed for thirty years and has been refurbished to its' previous art deco state which is all very Retro.

The evening did have a dampner on it though as is often the case here.

Before the film we went to a great local fish restaurant.

We got the last table so it was really loud and busy. During our meal Abbie rang me on my mobile to ask what time we would be home. The young woman on the table behind us became very aggressive and tried to demand I got off the phone!!!

Naturally she got flicked the 'bird' but it was just so un-necessary but people here are just SO intolerant! One of my friends was at toys R Us recently, here they still have all the sweets by the checkout. Her 2 year old kicked off in the queue demanding sweets and threw a 2 year old paddy when told NO. Well, the woman standing behind my friend threatened to call the police!! Lovely lady, very helpful…

To-day Nige went into work and the kids and I went and got the ferry into San Fran to meet him. We got the guide book out as we wanted to do some more exploring of the city as we don't get the chance that often. It really is a fabulous city. Did you know that San Fran actually has less than a million people which is sod all for an International city. I always feel very safe here. I have also just read '1906' by James Dellassandro which is a novel about the 1906 earthquake that almost totally destroyed the city bar a handful of buildings.

We went for lunch in little Italy and then decided to walk to the top of Telegraph hill which has the most amazing views of the city. Ben took his camera which promptly ran out of batteries as we reached the top I did not need to go to the gym tonight as walking up those hills is a killer. At the top there is a weird looking tower building made to look like the end of a Firemans hose and was built to honour the cities volunteer firemen and is known as Coit tower. How anyone EVER decided to build houses on these hills amazes me. Must have been a bloody man..

Now, I don't know if anyone has read the book or seen the film called 'The Parrots Of Telegraph Hill', but they were my inspiration for walking to the top.

Apparently there are a flock of parrots, about 50, that have been in San Francisco for over 40 years and no-ones knows where they came from or how they survive.

Well, we saw nowt…until we were making our way back to the ferry building and cut through a little park where we heard the most almighty racket and there they were! All of them with green bodies and red heads, there was a Park Ranger there who told us that they could be found there most afternoons. Bloody guide book didn't mention that!

On the way back to the ferry I planned our next visit to see the amazing mansions built during the Gold boom where the likes of Danielle Steel and the Getty family now live.

After all the recent flooding which is still very much in evidence the weather has been great for the last two weeks so I have been out walking and biking with the kids. This Wednesday Nige is in New York so I plan to have some girlies over for some chilli, chat and Californian red so that should be fun.

Other than that things are ticking over, the time seems to go so quickly and I am starting to realize that I need to find us somewhere else to live really soon. I have met a great girl who lives further up the mountain to me who also rents but thinks she will be moving away in July. Her house would be great but she gets snakes in her pool and coyotes in the garden and I am not sure I can face that!

February 4th, 2006

BLUE ARSED FLY...

That is exactly what I have been like the last few weeks! We decided we had better pull our fingers out and plan everything we want to do before we leave and book it all in one go. Consequently we shall be having a fantastic year. We plan to go skiing again in Squaw Valley, in May we are off to San Luis Obispo which is on the way to L.A and is a really pretty seaside town with lots to do. In July we have booked to go to one of the Hawaiian Islands called Kauai and stay in a little place right on the beach where there is naff all to do except read and snorkel.

Somewhere in between all this we need to move house again. I have found us a great house near the kids' schools, on the flats, so the kids can bike to school and generally have a lot more freedom and independence. The big bonus for me is not having to do the 2 hour school run! What will I do with my day?

Last week Abbie and I went to listen to a speaker at her school. His name was David Roche and he has a severe facial deformity and came to school to talk to the kids about what it is like to be a kid at school and look so different. He was brilliant, I had a chat to him afterwards and he is about to embark on a tour of England and is starting in Liverpool or Cardiff. Apparently he appears on TV quite a lot here. If you get the chance to go and see him do go. He is very funny and charismatic. I think he was asked to speak at the school as a young girl has just started there with what I suspect is Aperts Syndrome.

We had a bizarre day yesterday, at 7am all the power went off. Nige was due to fly to Japan that morning. I went to take the kids to school, when I got to the bottom of our drive the Sheriff was parked across it blocking my way! I got out to ask him why and he yelled at me to get back in the car! The overhead power cable had fallen into the road and was bouncing live in the middle of it. The poor Sheriff was frantically trying to stop people from driving over it! As a result Nigel missed his flight and had to get a later one and the kids missed the morning in school until it was all fixed!

This week-end was frantic, this morning I coached the boys' soccer team, thank-god they won or I would never have lived it down! It was an intense match and my only sub started barfing 5 minutes into the game!

After the game it was a quick lunch and then I drove the boys to a party sleepover at a house on the beach which is a really windy drive that takes the best part of an hour. Then I dropped Abbie off at her party sleepover and then Leo and I went off for a walk with the dog. So tonight its home alone for Leo and I! In the morning I have to go and get the boys, drive them to another party, and then go and get Abbie, take her to a soccer game and then go and get the boys again and then I have invited a friend over for dinner with her 4 kids! Actually, she is a really interesting girl, she's Irish but has been here for 12 years and she writes crime novels set in Victorian Ireland. Pretty cool!

The weather is lovely and warm again, so much so the lizards are coming out after months of hiding!

I did have a major Millie Tant moment this week AGAIN. One of Nigel's work colleagues, also European, lives near here. He and his wife had a baby 2 months ago and the poor bairn is colicky and so, to give his wife a break, he put the baby in the pram and started pounding the pavements. We all know what that's like, you either put them in the car and drive for miles or you wear out the soles of your shoes walking. Well, the poor man said there was a woman walking ahead of him who turned around, walked back to him and told him to,

"shut the f***ing baby up!"

This sort of attitude here drives me mad; it happens to me every couple of weeks.

I ended up writing huge letters to every American on my email list saying exactly what I thought about these types of people and how it is no wonder half the world hates them. I cannot describe to you how arrogant and nasty a lot of people here are.

Someone recently said that what we have here are the offspring of the hippie movement whose parents blamed all their problems on the Government or other people and were brought up to believe that everything was someone elses' fault and not theirs. The result being a generation who say what they want, sue anyone who does not do what they want and take no responsibility for their own actions. I hear it time and time again, on the street and even in school. A perfect stranger here will think nothing of yelling at your children to 'shut up'; in front of you and no-one does anything back for fear of litigation.

Well, in my email I said if I meet yet another one of these types I was going to make them swallow their own teeth and wake up the following week in the Intensive Care Unit. This of course would make me just as bad as them and I'd end up in jail.

Anyway, enough ranting. Am off to bed with a cuppa and the latest book, this one is 'The birth of Venus', can't remember the author!

March 2nd, 2006

GREETINGS FROM THE POLICE STATE

Greetings y'all, hope you are all well and heading into Spring. We have had some right queer weather here I can tell you or maybe it's just the 'Fiona curse'. We had two weeks of fab weather, back into shorts and t shirts, sun cream and hats…this is what I told our friends who were coming to us from the UK via a ski stop in Minnesota and, who were really looking forward to some sunshine! I was rather embarrassed to tell them the day before they arrived that I had ice on the car for the first time since we have been here!

Having said all that, the weather was mild whilst they were here if not a little wet on their second day. We had a wonderful time with them all. It made me realize how long it has been since I laughed so hard I blew snot bubbles and cried hysterically at the same time!

A few days prior to their arrival we had some sad news at school. One of the Dads had shot himself in the chest and died instantly. He was one of these men who was always around and on every committee going and at every party. Sadly, it seems he was suffering from depression that even his wife didn't realize he was taking medication for.

Part of me feels very angry, he did it at home with his kids playing outside and his wife downstairs, she was taken in for questioning for several hours. Those poor kids will never get over this and you wonder if this will trigger history to repeat itself in years to come. I sincerely hope not.

On a lighter note, the kids have had a week off school and the weather warmed back up. We have had a great chilling out week and have been off hiking, going to the health club to swim and play basketball and having friends over. We also spent a fab day on the beach with the kids and pals building a dam and me sat curled up with Raffy and a book, bliss! I shall miss moments like these, especially in mid February.

The soccer is going well, we have one more week left of indoor soccer before the Spring league starts for outside! Next week-end we have the tryouts for the 'Select Team' which the three older ones have been advised to try out for. We put it off last year as it is a huge commitment but Nige feels that as this is our last year we should let them go for it.

Last year 50 kids were put through, but only 20 made it, so I imagine it will be an emotional 2 days. The hardship of twins is if one gets through and the other doesn't, but then that's life I suppose.

Poor Nigel is feeling very morose to-day as one of the agreements to us staying another year was that he had to get rid of the two seater Audi convertible…it is such a nightmare at week-ends trying to ferry kids about. So, to-day he sold the TT and got…an A4 5 seater convertible instead!

And yes, he does still have the 'Death Machine' as well!

We are gradually building up to moving house although things are a bit stressful as the owners of this house have now decided to sell this house and not move in themselves. The downside of this is that every man and his bloody dog keep coming over to view. Selling a property here is SO very different from home. Let me try to explain.

Firstly, Marin County has a no new build property law. Therefore, there are 4,000 estate agents chasing previously owned houses. In this area the average house price is $850,000 and the agents charge 6% commission!

You don't have to sell many houses a year to do OK here!

Imagine, this house is on the market for $2.3 million, you can expect to sell your house within 60 days. After that time it is called a sitting duck! As a result of all this we are getting a bit depressed as there seems to be people here all the time. When a house is first put up for sale they have 2 Open House days, where anyone can wander through for a look around. The first Open House is for all the local Estate agents to come and view the house and then report back to their clients. The second is for the public to come and view the house.

I have already had a row with one agent who phoned up wanting to bring in a 'stager', apparently this involved putting OUR stuff in to storage and putting in trendy minimalist rented furniture. I did have to point out to her that we do pay rent to live here and that it was our home until the day we moved out and she was not moving anything!

On that note, we hope to be in our new house by July 1st but we still have no definite date and now I don't know whether to look for something else or hope that it all pans out. The problem is this seems such a good deal, it is a little smaller than this but right by the schools and a good deal cheaper in rent.

I did laugh this week though maybe I shouldn't. Apparently, a woman was 'attacked' whilst hiking on one of my fave walks. She was walking along and a bloke passed her on his bike. She felt it was her right to inform him that bikes were not allowed on the trail and that she was going to report him to the police. He then apparently, gave her a hefty shove into the nearest bush where she landed on her arse! Personally I think he should be given a bloody medal!

So, it's Sunday night, the kids are back to school tomorrow, its raining outside and the only kids sleeping here are my own! Last night I had an 11 year old, a ten year old, five nine year olds and two two year olds!

Nigel left at 5:30 am to find a bar in the city where he witnessed Wales receive a complete licking by Ireland in the rugby!

March 12th, 2006

IS IT A CROCK OF SHITE OR A COCKAPOO?

Please tell me the craze for mixing perfectly good breeds of dogs and giving them ridiculous names has not spread over the pond? Everywhere I go here I see 'new' breeds of dogs and always get the giggles when I ask what breed they are.

Over here they call dogs like Raffy 'hypoallergenic', to us they are just dogs that don't shed or molt. Well, someone with too much time on their hands and a vivid imagination has been playing God. There are some right queer looking mutts in the park

Cock – a-poo – this is a cross between a cocker spaniel and a poodle.

Labradoodle- a cross between a Labrador and a poodle

Retri- doodle – a retriever cross with a poodle

Only in America, bloody nutters

if you crossed Raffy with a poodle would you get a Tibitapoo I wonder?!!

The last two weeks have been busy, no surprise there then! Last week-end and this one the boys have had their 'tryouts' for the select soccer team. The competition is very tough as there are very few places and even if they played last year they still have to try out again to secure their place. It's all very professional.

Interestingly, the parents are kept well away from the pitch so they cannot harass the coaches or try to influence them. Many of these parents try to push their kids into these teams in the hope that the child can then get a scholarship into University. It seems madness to me to push them now for something in nine years that they may not want to pursue. We should get the phone call with the results tonight or tomorrow...

Nige will bloody kill me if they don't get in as the TT went yesterday; I thought he was going to cry!!

Last Monday I had the first of my Mineral Body Wraps that Nigel had bought me for Christmas. I tell you, you have never seen anything like it. I was wrapped from head to foot in bandages, literally, and then hosed down with minerals. I was then put on a treadmill for an hour, I nearly wet myself laughing trying to imagine what would happen if the fire alarm went off and the staff ran out and left me! The bandages chaffed my bum and my arms were bandaged so tightly they stuck at right angles to my body so I couldn't reach the machine to turn it off!

I was in agony but laughing so hard, the assistant was in the next room on the phone to her boyfriend and had left a DVD on really loud so she couldn't hear me.

I've got to go through that another five times!

Last Saturday the boys went to a party with an illusionist. One little boy was sick and 72 hours later all eight of the little darlings were puking. By the Tuesday Sam and Ben were lying with buckets either side of them and I was disinfecting the house from top to bottom. I was up to my arms in my marigolds and bleach when the soon to be new house owner turned up with her mother, a surveyor and a pest controller!

I can assure you the house did not smell of coffee and freshly baked bread...

In a few weeks the boys are off on a school trip up to the gold country where they stay in an old mining village and go into the river and pan for gold, how cool is that?

On the 24th we are all off ski-ing, the kids are hoping to see me peeing into the back of my shoes at the side of the road again...

Speaking of peeing, Leo has now mastered potty training, I however, have not.

Our downstairs loo looks like a disabled bathroom with two steps up to the bog, a raised seat with handlebars plus a step up to the sink!

I have now remembered to put a spare potty in the car. The other day I was on the equivalent of the M1 when Leo shouted

"Need pee mummy".

When I got to the underground car park at my destination that changed to

"Need poo mummy".

I'd like to take this opportunity to apologise to anyone who parked in spot 23 on California Street…..

On Wednesday Nigel had his eyes lasered. It is pretty amazing and took less than a minute per eye. Very expensive minutes at $2,000 a go!

Nige did say though, that rather than have it done again he would prefer the vasectomy without the anaesthetic. Ouch!

On Saturday it was the coldest day recorded here since 1950 and there was a chance of snow, there is some already on the very top of the mountain. I fully expect to be deported any time soon...

Raffy is very miserable at the moment, he hates going to the groomers; they charge a small fortune too and are miserable sods to boot. He desperately needed doing so I had the bright idea of buying a $10 pair of clippers and doing him myself. Four hours later he looks like a rat, I nicked his neck so he is wearing a lampshade on his head and is sat in his basket shaking. I guess the miserable woman deserves the $90 after all.

I'll call her in the morning...

March 31st, 2006

RECORD BREAKER

Well, if it rains again tomorrow this will officially be the wettest March recorded here since 1805. It has now pissed down for twenty six sodding consecutive days!

I am even getting a reputation here for having the bad weather curse. You remember I booked for us to go to Hawaii? The other night Nigel and I were on the computer when we heard the news on TV in the other room. Apparently there have been freak flash floods on Kauai and the dam burst its banks and wiped out hundreds of buildings. Of all the Hawaiian Islands what are the chances of that happening to the one little one that I managed to book a holiday on?

Nige says we are moving to somewhere in Africa, or did he say just I was?

A happy belated Saint Patricks' day to all you Irish. Bless the Californians, any excuse to party. There were loads of parties and parades here. One of Bens' friends kindly invited us all round for a Paddy day dinner. We had the whole works, corned beef hash, white cabbage, Irish soda bread, the lot. We were too embarrassed to say we're not Irish but I think the wife may have guessed when she asked me who Saint Patrick was and why is he famous and I stood umming and arring and looking pleadingly at Nigel who remained oblivious to my discomfort!

What was even more bizarre but great was this family are Jewish and so we had Shabbat with them where they lit the candles whilst saying Hebrew prayers prior to scoffing the Irish dinner. We had a lovely night, lots of wine and good conversation. The wife used to live in England in the 1980's but got deported when the authorities found out she was working illegally. She was caught out by keeping a diary that was read at the airport when she returned to the UK after visiting family out here.

She has a really cool job; she is a 'gemologist' and designs jewelry for the Hollywood celebs!

We had our ski-ing trip last week-end. We went off to the Sierra Nevada Mountains to Squaw Valley. The first day we had the most horrific storm but after that it was really hot and we all got a bit of dodgy goggle burn. This time we even got Leo on a pair of ski's and into ski school. He just loved it and we had a job to get him off the snow!

This morning Jenn came over with her party organizer, she is having her 40th birthday party here at our house. She will be having a cocktail bar, D.J and casino table and a henna tattoo artist!

All Leo gets for his birthday next week is a bouncy castle and a jam butty.

Sam is starting a cookery course next week, move over Mr. Oliver; I hope he is more a Jamie than that gobshite Gordon!

Well, it's peeing down again, there are 5 snails on the window as I type. Yuck!

Go on, tell me the weather there is lovely and the Daffs are out?

April 11th, 2006

AND IT IS STILL RAINING...

Well, the record for the most rain to ever fall in Marin County has now been well and truly broken. It has now rained, more or less, for five months and almost non stop for the last thirty six days. I cannot tell you how depressing it is when there is so little to do here when the weather is bad. All the kids extra curricular activities are cancelled because they are all based outside. Cabin fever just isn't in it!

We had Leos' third birthday party here on Sunday with 16 two and three year olds plus siblings. We were able to drag the bouncy castle under the awning so the kids could run from the house onto it without getting wet! Leo was somewhat bewildered by the whole day and kept asking when they were all going home.

Some lessons in social etiquette needed there! Like last year only five from his school turned up, at least this year I knew more people to make up for it. The locals are so rude about invitations and often just don't show up without bothering to let you know.

This past two weeks has seen two more 'incidents', one of which makes me doubt that I can stick it out another year. We went into SanFran to a science museum that we had recently got memberships for. After we left we went out for dinner. On the way back to the car Nigel was walking ahead with 2 kids and I was walking behind with the other two, having a chat about what we had seen that day. The next moment a man slams into Abbie knocking her to the ground and walks off! I shouted after him

"Why the hell did you just do that?"

He turned back to me and said

"Single fucking file lady, single fucking file".

This was an average middle aged white American walking along a quiet street at 7pm with his wife/partner.

Bastard.

The second time, the weather had dried up for an hour so Leo and I took Raffy to the park. Leo was on the swing and Raffy was on a lead tucked under my foot. A toddler came towards us and her pregnant mother started running towards me screaming. Well, I thought something was seriously wrong and called to ask if she needed help. The next thing is she trying to pull the lead from under my foot and drag Raffy away! A second later her husband joins in along with another woman, who five minutes before had asked if her toddler could stroke Raffy. Eventually I got the lead off them and asked them what the hell they were doing. They were having a fit because there was a dog near children and were trying to drag him out the park!

Mad, the lot of them.

Moan over, for now.

As far as the house sale here goes it is all quite depressing. The people who were suppose to be buying it now aren't and it has gone back on the market so there is now a constant stream of people walking through the house. Even as I type there are cars racing up the drive for a quick peek and then driving off again. I have put a sign up saying 'children play here', but it got run over! I have stopped the kids from playing in front of the house now.

Next Thursday is Open House day again for the agents and open again the following week for the public. It's like living in a gold fish bowl. I wish we could move out sooner but we can't.

How pleased I am to have downloaded the next series of 'No Angel', just what I need to cheer me up. I did have a good laugh the other day though, in true Fiona humour.

Remember I wrote about the Dad that recently shot himself? Well, one of the schools upcoming fundraiser is to be a golf tournament with teams of four.

Some of the mums were talking about it at school, including the new widow who asked one of the other mums if her brother would be interested in joining her team of three women.

"Oh god no. He'd rather shoot himself than play golf", she replied.

There was a hideous silence then someone piped up

"What kind of golf are we playing anyway?"

Shotgun came the reply!

AND, none of it was said by me.

The other thing that has given me a laugh over the last few weeks has been Ben's teachers' blogg. Mrs. Aubert is a fantastic teacher and a definite rebel! The other teachers, especially the female ones hate her I'm sure. Her nickname is Ms. Woody, so named by the male fraternity!

At the end of the school year she is leaving to become a full time comedienne. As mentioned before she has this blogg which is all very professionally done. She does not talk about it unless you know her pretty well. It is not the sort of blogg address that you would stumble across. This has not stopped one of the particularly anally retentive mums at the school from insisting that the school administration force her to close her blogg. This particular mum is what I now call a 'helicopter' parent. She has one child and fawns over him completely. She is at the school as much as possible and the poor child can't sneeze without her being there to wrap him in cotton wool. Poor kid can't even go on a school trip because she is so paranoid. Thanks to her the school brought in lawyers to force Mrs. Aubert to close her blogg.

Have a look for yourself. I particularly liked a recent entry about the 'bearded clam'. Personally I have always called mine my Majorca, Minorca and my Cyprus...

I will leave you with that thought!

www.growingoutmybangs.com

28th April, 2006

RANT, MOAN AND RAVE

I feel that's all I've done in the last few newsletters. The last two weeks have been like a roller coaster, up and down. We have had some great days out; I bought four kites from the bargain bin and took the kids to a beach just off the Golden Gate Bridge. We spent a good two hours flying them, or rather the kids did. I spent the time huddled under Leo's blanket because I was so cold!

We did a tour ride in one of the popular motorized trolley carts around the city for two hours. We drove past Danielle Steeles' house called Spreckles Mansion; it was owned by one of the richest men from the Gold rush era in 1849. The whole area is called Pacific Heights and is the steepest part of the city. The houses are just amazing but not an old person in sight! The trolley carts were designed by a Scot called John Hamilton who took pity on the horses trying to pull the building materials up the steep hills.

We went past the house where the movie Mrs. Doubtfire was filmed; Robin Williams actually lives in SanFran. The tour took us through Golden Gate Park and past the new studios of George Lucas; R2D2 can be seen standing on guard. It was a great way to see lots and learn a bit more about the city. Coming from a Roman city it fascinates me that San Fran only really dates back to 1849. Our cottage in England was built in 1825!

April 19th marked the hundred year anniversary of the big 1906 Earthquake. There has been a lot written about it and re-enactments to visit. Of course, all the seismologists are trying to predict when the next biggie will happen and put the fear of God into us.

I have now come to the conclusion that there are only two seasons here. Bloody hot and bloody wet! One day last week the rain stopped, I turned off the heating. The next day we were all in shorts and I am nagging the kids to slap on the sun bloc!

Sam and Ben's school trip to the Gold Country was cancelled because of the rain, they hope to go in May now. They were really disappointed, poor lambs. We had another week-end ski-ing. The boys are now on the black runs on snowboards and Abbie is on them on skis. I had another two hour lesson and despite spending vast amounts of time on my arse or face down eating the white stuff I have at least now managed a couple of runs in the upright position! I rather think I look like Renee Zelweger in the scene from the Edge of Reason when Colin Firth asks her if she can get down the mountain on her own. She's dressed up like the Easter bunny and kind of hurtles herself down the mountain and through the hotel revolving doors before smacking in to the reception desk...

I do enjoy going up there, the only thing that gets on my pip is that we always bump into one of Nigel' work colleagues and end up feeling obliged to meet up for dinner with them. Wherever you go here you always see the same faces, despite the fact that we are 3 hours from home. Last year in Yosemite National Park the boys saw a kid from their class!

This time we drove up to the snow at night time and I was driving. The conditions can be quite scary and there are no road markings or lights. I came round one corner approaching the resort and was head on to another car, we had both misjudged the road width. Am not sure who was more scared but I could see the whites of his eyes!

We have had to get another car this week as the other one was on a two year rental that has now expired. This new one is sending me nuts. Everything is electrical, doors, windows and the boot. As I'm driving along the kids keep pressing the buttons so the windows are all going up and down. When we have been shopping I have twice nearly knocked someone out. As I approach the car the boot opens, if someone is walking past and not looking up then they get thwacked by my boot door! The worst part is the school run, when we do car duty the cars that have electric doors take so long to open and close that they cause a huge queue and I am the worst one for moaning about them. I couldn't believe it when Nigel came home with this one; I have taken to parking in the disabled spot at school to let the kids out!

This house has now sold for $2.185 million! I have had rather a lot of problems with 'Pushy Patty', the estate agent who has taken to letting herself in with a key!

The other day I was standing doing the ironing whilst watching a film and in she walked with two people. The next minute there were six couples wandering in the front door! She totally ignored me, walked into the kitchen and moved my things off the dining table and laid out some architect plans!

We ended up in a shouting match, for once I did not cry in total frustration but stood and gave as good as I got. I was rather proud of myself for telling her she reminded me of a little dog nipping at my heels and was in need of a swift kick up the arse to make her let go!

As you can imagine things have rather deteriorated with the owners because of this. It is a real shame as they were often here for a chat and a cup of tea but the situation has become intolerable. We received a letter from them saying that if we were not out by June 1st then they would double our rent! I had to speak to a lawyer because our rental contract is until July. Abbie and I were very childish, we defaced all of Pushy Patty's calling cards that she leaves for viewers. We drew horns and fangs on all but the top one! Petty I know but nothing compared to how low she has stooped!

To-day is Friday, thank goodness! Sam is cooking tea, the cover is on the pool to heat it up, and the wine is chilling.

I rather wish Pushy Patty was face down under the cover...

May 11th, 2006

ON TOP OF OLE SMOKEY

Ten days ago I had the heating on full blast and everywhere was lush green, many places still had the tarpaulin covering the mudslide areas. In that short time the weather has whacked up to 85 degrees and everything is turning yellow.

Hence the reason it is called the Golden State, only it's not golden, it's just dead!

Lots of us are walking round looking like lobsters, because there is no Spring, as such, your body does not have time to acclimatize to the sun. The poor kids have been playing footie in 90 degrees as all of their matches are further inland where it is even hotter. We had our first parent meeting of the 'select team', yes, all three of them made it!! In true Fiona fashion Nige parked the car and I got out and stepped in a pile of dog poo…in my open toe sandals. Not nice…

Despite no-one wanting to sit near me they were a nice bunch of parents. I spent half an hour filling in forms and writing cheques while Nigel talked 'shop' with all the Dads!

The boys returned yesterday from the school trip up in the Gold country where they went wading in rivers panning for gold and visited the cabins used by the real gold miners from the mid 1800's. They had a great time, the school provided the parents with a phone number so that we could ring and listen to a message recorded by the kids telling us what they had been doing that day. It was very interesting to note the large number of kids that did not go; noticeably most of these were single child families with mega over protective parents. It is such a shame, I feel, because all the other kids are raving about what a great time they all had and these kids are left out. Apparently the parents who did not let their kids go were worried that the teachers would hold it against the kids. I would think it more likely that the kids would hold it against their parents!

As you can imagine our house was really quiet with two gone, I tell you what do you lot moan about with just two kids at home? Piece of cake that was!

Last Sunday we had a fab night, some friends of ours live in the last road on the mountain with houses on. They are fun people who are originally from here but have been living in Boston for the last ten years. They came back here for his job but have been back for almost a year but hate it, so they are moving back to Boston at the end of July. See, it's not just me!

Anyway, the view from their rented house is stunning; the hubby plays golf from the shed roof and hits the balls into infinity from there! We were sat outside having a BBQ and, as the sun set on top of the mountain, the coyotes started their evening calls. It is incredible to listen to, we can't hear them from our house. It made the hairs on the back of my neck stand up. I don't think I will ever hear that again.

Abbie has been the sporty queen at school and was chosen to run the 600 metres at what they call a track meet where all the local schools compete against each other on a huge outdoor track. She was in her element as she loves running…usually away from me! Tomorrow night she if off to the Oakland arena to a Black Eyed Peas concert with twelve girlfriends in a private box no less! I should be so lucky.

Little Leo has been very poorly recently, last Thursday he developed Croup really badly in the night. We spent the night in the shower room with him to help him breathe but he got so bad he ended up on steroids and in a tent with a humidifier blowing moist air in. He is now much better and has finished the steroids and is down the gym pumping iron in front of the mirror wearing Lycra shorts……not.

This week I have two positive things to tell you!!

ONE) all parents from school were sent an email regarding the release of nine paedophiles from San Quentin Prison along with their photos and a copy of a phone call between the Sheriff and the school explaining how long these animals will be living in our community. They also provided a website that you can log onto to identify where any registered abusers live along with details of their crimes and recent personal photos of the abuser. This is all a result of Megans' Law but apparently this is not allowed in all the states.

TWO) a large amount of money went missing from my account. We informed the bank which immediately cancelled my card, paid us back the missing money and launched a fraud inquiry without a single doubt or question. That was impressive service.

This week sees me alone as Nige is off to Japan and so I am left to ferry kids to footie matches and provide the taxi service to the kids' various social engagements! I am, however, off to a friends' house tomorrow for a girlie night. Am slightly worried as last time I saw the host at a party she staggered over and grabbed my boobs and 'honked' them…do I hope that doesn't happen again!

I'll let you know.

Sam and Ben on the tow path between the two schools.

May 29th, 2006

HOLA WITH THE FUNNY HYPHEN BIT OVER THE A….!

Hola to you all, I hope you are all better than my crappy Spanish! We have had a busy few weeks as school draws to an end, I find it hard to believe how fast this school year has gone. The kids have now almost completed their second full school year here. It officially ends on June 16th, after that the three older kids will all be at the same school which makes my life even easier!

At this time of year the schools have a massive drive to raise all the last minute funds, so, every week there is something going on. Last week should have been 'family fun day' with races, best dog competition and dunk the teacher BUT for the first time in one hundred years the forecast was for rain! Consequently it was re-scheduled. Is it me or what?

This time of year leaves me feeling knackered as I volunteer for all three schools and, quite frankly, I often forget what I have been badgered into volunteering for until I get a phone call reminding me. As a result I run round helping out doing gardening, cooking, chaperoning discos, cleaning up after parties and ferrying hideous amounts of ungrateful brats from one place to another…usually my own!

Last Friday night I was asked to chaperone the 6th, 7th, and 8th Grade disco, I did have a laugh! I was stuck in the kitchen helping serve drinks and snacks but I kept sneaking off for a peek. I was mortified to find my daughter slow dancing with the school 'beau' but, I had to bite my tongue and said nowt until she told me. Not like me at all that is it?!

Next, for the boys, it is the end of year swim party where the school rent a fab pool for all the kids that are leaving the school before moving onto Middle school. They put on a huge BBQ and all the kids get a white T shirt to sign their pals' names on. I am down to help supervise that too!

This week-end was Memorial Day so on Friday we took off in the car down to San Luis Obispo; this is about half way between San Fran and Los Angeles along the Californian coastline. This road is known as the Camino Real and it is the road that linked all twenty one of the Missions' that formed the towns and cities of California. We stayed at an Inn just outside the town that we used as a base. We visited Hearst Castle which is a stunning mansion built on an 'enchanted' hill by William Randolph Hearst who was a publishing / media/ movie tycoon of the 1920's / 30's. Or, in fact, if you Google him he won the land in a card game and was a Nazi sympathizing womanizer! The house is incredibly lavish and was the ultimate place to be invited to if you were part of the 'IT' group of those times.

We spent a lovely day at Avila Beach which was six miles south of our Inn. San Luis is a really lovely seaside community, we have found a lot of what we would call traditional towns south of San Fran, and I do wish we had settled in one of these.

They are much friendlier and community based and so much more like home really. Speaking of which, we met a great English girl there from Weymouth. We made each other feel homesick and she has been here for eleven years!

We came back to an answer phone message from the Moving Company saying they would be here at 8am tomorrow morning… …a whole month before they should be!

This coming week-end sees our dear friend Jenns' 40th Birthday party here. She has pulled out all the stops, apparently she knows a lot of 'Hollywood Gay Luvvie types so that should completely freak Nigel out for the evening then!

More next week on that one!

June 11th, 2006

A DOSE OF NORMALITY

And what a wonderful dose it was to be sure to be sure! Yesterday we headed off to San Jose (was it Dion Warwick that sang asking for directions?) to watch a Rugby match! San Jose is just over an hours drive south of San Fran and is a very affluent Colonial type town that made its money during the Dot.Com era, loads of companies made it their headquarters so, as a result, it is a very funky but smart town.

Nigel had been watching the rugby on TV and seeing as the weather here was cloudy he decided it would be fun to head south for some sun. The rugby was at Santa Clara University and it was the Rugby Churchill Cup that was being played. We were to see Ireland A play the New Zealand Maoris'. What an absolute laugh the day was. Sat next to us was a bus load of Irish lads who have been living and working in San Fran for six months. Totally defying the California laws they sat chain smoking their Marlboros' and necking pint after pint of Guinness and singing at the top of their voices. Every other word out of their mouthes was 'fuck' as they yelled at the Refs. At one point, one of them caught the ball after a drop kick. They made the poor preppie boy who came to retrieve it lifes' hell. Every single one of them were wearing a white T shirt, each time preppie asked them who had the ball they all pointed at each other and shouted

"The fecker in the white shirt has it".

It was such a great atmosphere with lots of singing and Mexican waves; I thought I was back in Watford watching the Saracens play against the Wasps! There was even an old boy with a knotted white hankie on his head, the few Yanks that were there must have been mind boggled!

As well as going there yesterday our house has of course been full of World Cup Fever. At 6am yesterday all the boys were up and some friends arrived to watch what we thought was a very dull match between Paraguay and England. I did take great delight in phoning the boys' French teacher and gloating about Englands' victory though! Nigel is off to Germany for the England V Sweden game as a freebie!

Talking of Nige, we were rather horrified this week to have been asked for a $1,000 'donation' to pay for a birthday present for his boss! Apparently, some people in his office decided, in a very brown nose, kind of way that they would buy him a friggin' Harley Davidson bike, customized with all their names engraved upon it!! We were only told after the deed was done!! I hope Nigel gets a bloody big bonus to make up for it!

Last week was our friend Jenns' 40th party here. It was a fun night, I could not believe the work that went into it. They were a great crowd of people from every walk of life. There was a Hollywood producer, a writer of a newspaper column and some would be luvvies!

My dining room was a Poker hall, there was a DJ outside plus a full bar. Five people serving amazing food and a henna tattoo artist circling the crowd. It was my kind of party, no babysitter (kids stayed at Jenns with hers), no cab fare home and no cost at all! Other people set up and other people cleared away! There was a very camp entertainer, Binky the Elf, and lots of dancing. This house is just perfect for huge parties. There were even hundreds of candles floating in the pool.

The only sad, but not really surprising part was that a neighbour called the police who arrived at 10:30 pm and said that the music had to be off by 11pm.

Considering we can't even see a neighbours house from ours I thought it was a bit Draconian but that's Marin County for you!

Needless to say the only single girl went home with the Poker dealer and the remaining drunkards ended up semi naked in the pool at some unearthly hour!

To-day was the school family fun day, it started with a Fun Run of a mile along the tow path between the two schools, which the kids made me do! After that it was huge bouncy castles or Jumpees as they call them here. There were bands playing and a BBQ. I did my bit volunteering on the water tag ride, a bit like Quasar but wetter!

So, schools out on Friday. I have spent the week going to every event possible. I have cooked lunches, looked after seven two year olds, supervised 300 eleven years olds at a dance, driven hideous amounts of ten year olds and am now horribly knackered. In between all this I have tried to pack for us moving house on June 30th! This in itself may be a nightmare, I had a phone call from our future landlord saying the present tenants are refusing to move out and he has served them with an eviction notice…I feel a bad moment coming on.

I am now on countdown until I come home in August. That will be the first time I have been home since Feb 2005. By the time we move into the new house (hopefully) it will be less than a year until we are home for good!

July 21st, 2006

ALOHA!

A big Hawaiian hello to you all!

We have had a very fraught three weeks which ended with the perfect holiday.

We were under tremendous pressure to move out of Hillbilly House by the 1st of July as the new owners wanted to move in the same day. All went well up to a point, the week before we were due to move into the new place I called the then tenants to ask if Nige and the kids could go and see the house as, up until then only I had seen it. The tenant agreed to meet us at the house. When we arrived the place was empty and it was obvious no-one was living there. I therefore asked when it would be convenient to her for me to start bringing a few bits over. She said that as she had paid the rent up until the 31st then the 31st was the earliest!

The actual day of the move went well, the T.V was the last thing to go as, much to the disgust of the rest of my family I had chosen the day of the final match of the World Cup to move house. Oops!

The guys who moved us were a great laugh, however, they did manage to pack our bags meant for us to stay in a hotel overnight! That evening, once everything was loaded onto the vans ready to be delivered the next day, we went to Jenns house for tea.

At 9pm it suddenly occurred to me that we did not have a key to get into the new house! When I called the landlord he told me the previous tenants had said that as they had paid the rent up until midnight on the 31st then that was when we would get the keys!

I have to say that the next morning I must have looked like a hooker, the only luggage we had was a bag of ironing in which I found a pair of Bens' underpants!

So, at 7am I left the hotel with a plastic bag containing my knickers from the day before, wearing 10 year olds underwear whilst the rest of the buggers watched the footie on the hotel T.V!

Anyway, the house looked great despite the fact that the previous tenant, the evil cow, had not left the keys in the arranged place so I had to break in through the garage!

So far it has been fantastic, the neighbours have all been over to say hello, and one of them is from Wiltshire! The kids have enjoyed being able to play out in the cul-de-sac on their bikes. One of Abbies' friends from school lives next door but one. Think Wisteria Lane meets Brookside Close and your there...

After a week of blistering heat (98 plus) and unpacking boxes we went off on holiday to the island of Kauai.

We had the most wonderful ten days. Kauai is the 4th largest of the Hawaiian Islands of which there are eight and is the 50th State of America. It is a tropical island and is officially the wettest place on earth! So it's not bloody Cornwall after all, and, I have to say it did rain most days. It is 33 miles by 25 miles and is known as the Garden Island as it is so green and lush. When it did rain it was hot rain and lasted a very short time. We had a self catering apartment with a view over the ocean and a private beach with a lovely pool. We could walk almost everywhere. We were SO lucky that a 'Monk' seal came to rest on our beach. These seals are solitary, there are less than 1300 left in the world and only 16 – 30 of them on this island and are fiercely protected. She stayed for nearly 24 hours, all 900lbs of her.

You can imagine our disgust when some dreadful Americans asked the officials to move her off the beach because they wanted to use the beach that they had paid for!!

Unbelievable.

One day, Nigel and the three older kids went off Snuba diving. As opposed to Scuba diving your oxygen tank is on a floating raft with an air pipe connected to it allowing you to dive up to twenty feet, with an instructor, without having to do a diving certificate. The dive was for thirty minutes and they got to hand feed the fish and it was all recorded on DVD for them to keep.

On another day, the kids and I had a helicopter tour over the island for an hour, it was amazing. As well as these, the kids and Nige went on a two hour horse riding trek and we all went for a dive in a cave called the Blue Room. This is a cave you climb down into and there is a large natural pool. Once in the pool you duck under a rock lip to an annex room where the sunshine illuminates the cave to a soft blue!

There are so many films made here, Jurassic Park, South Pacific, Blue Hawaii, Raiders of the Lost Ark and who remembers Fantasy Island? De plane boss, it da plane!

We had a fabulous time and it was truly lovely. The only thing that spoiled it for me was all the American fast food chains we saw everywhere. I know it is an American state but this did ruin the image of the island. The island was once owned by the Brits as there is a Union Jack on their flag and a mountain range known as Queen Victorias' Profile!

Despite this, we did not meet any other Brits but there were a whole lot of Aussies!

We arrived back at 6am this morning after out return flight with United Airlines.

Never in my whole life have I flown with a more dreadful airline. Apparently they are under severe financial pressure which is undoubtfully not helped by having the rudest most obnoxious unhelpful flight attendants we have yet come across! Don't get me started but this airline is unbelievably bad, even if you have flown with Monarch!

So, a good holiday was had by us all. It is now only eleven days until the kids and I fly (with lovely, lovely Virgin Airlines!) back to England for a months stay! We are so looking forward to seeing everyone. This will be our last 'return' before returning home for good!

View of Mount. Tam from the new house.

October 2nd, 2006

YON KIPPUR TO YOU ALL

Happy Jewish New Year! Due to the fact that 90% of all the kids at school are Jewish we have a long week-end off school to celebrate. I figure that if I go around all week saying Yon Kippur to everyone I see, and then in December I am justified in shouting Happy Christmas to the other 10%!

Whilst on the subject of Jews, I made our kids watch a great docu / film called Paperclips. It is a wonderfully moving and humbling film about a school in Tennessee which has no ethnic diversity at all. The decision is made to find a project about racism and prejudice and they decided to study the Holocaust. One of the school kids said he could not imagine what six million looked like (number of Jews that died) and so they decided to collect six million paperclips and what follows is amazing. I am a firm believer that films like Schindlers List and Paperclips should be compulsory viewing in all schools. Do get it and watch it with your kids, it triggers all sorts of discussions.

The rest of life is going well. I have now taken up jogging. I know it is hard to imagine a woman with a 40 inch chest, whom is normally associated with a glass of wine in one hand and a ciggie in the other, to take up running, but hey! The ciggies went two years ago, and I wear a sports bra so tight that I look like I have a giant watermelon attached to my chest and, lets face it, you have to put the wine glass down sometimes!

The girl I run with (the Irish Crime writer) has taken me on some wonderful local runs. One of them is called the Hoo Koo Ee Koo trail which is up on Mount Tam near our old house. It is simply stunning, I took Nige and the kids there over the week-end. It is an old Native American (Indians) cattle trail that circles the mountain.

The views are spectacular; Lena runs it on her own which I definitely would not do because of the Coyotes, Bobcats and Mountain Lions that roam up there. All of which you see more of now as the ground is so dry and therefore the deer (lion fodder!)

come further down the mountain into suburbia to find food and water and where Bambi goes, so follows Aslan!

I have actually been a 'working girl' this past two weeks which has been fun. A friend of ours, Jenn, is a real estate agent and has always raved about stagers, these are people who, once a house is put up for sale, do everything they can to make the house more attractive to prospective buyers. A bit like the program House Doctor.

I had often said to Jenn that I would love to have a go at doing a house up so she took me up on it! I was given a two bed empty house and a budget of $2,000 and was sent off to Ikea to buy bits and bobs like chairs and tables and lamps and rugs.

Well, I had a great three days doing it all up but hated putting the bloody Ikea furniture together. I always end up with several bits left over! I think that it was the first time I have been to Ikea and come back with something other than a potted plant and 500 tealights.

Yesterday was Open House where the public can wander through and apparently the other agents really liked what I had done. Maybe it is the start of a new job venture! How cool would that be? Get given loads of someone elses' money to buy what you want, make a house look funky and then get paid for it!

As I can't actually earn money here because of my visa restrictions I would have to get lots of gift vouchers instead, I can live with that!

Soccer season is in full swing, the boys had a game on Saturday. When we got home they told me that their coach, at half time, had a team chat and told the boys to cream the mother f***ers! Not sure how I'm going to handle that one yet. They lost 3:1 anyway!

Abbies' team remain undefeated. We have met a great new bloke whose daughter is on Abbies' team. Last week-end we had a huge BBQ for twenty two and invited him along. He has a tragic story. He was living in London for seven years working for a big high street bank, when you read this you might want to move your account! He had to return to the States two years ago because it was decided he was needed back here. However, he has had to leave his wife behind in England as she was involved in a terrible accident four years ago, that has left her in a coma ever since. She is too unwell to be moved and so poor Steve and his daughter had to leave her behind and move back here. What a wonderful compassionate bank, not!

Steve is a really fun bloke to be with and has a wicked sense of humour. When the girls are playing and the opposing team are winning he holds up signs that say 'tosser' and 'wanker'and no-ones knows what it means here!

Little Leo has started his Pee Wee soccer course on a Thursday morning and just loves it. He is so intense and hangs onto every word the coach says. It is so cute to see him as he runs round in his little Arsenal kit that Sam bought for him. I bought him a pair of trainers last week and told him they were cleats (footie boots) so he thinks he is the bees knees now! Last week he would only answer me if I called him Steven Gerrard! Poor Nigel has got no chance of him playing Rugby so I guess he is not going to live up to his middle name and no, I am NOT going to write that name down anywhere!

This month is of course Halloween which is just huge out here. I am gearing myself up to it big time as this area is where everyone descends to Trick and Treat as it is all on flat land. When selling a property around here you are required to sign a disclaimer saying that you accept to being swamped by kids at Halloween time! Seeing as this is our last one here we are going all out for it and having a big party. I have a wooden coffin, skulls and headstones for the front garden and started buying the sweets in bulk last month. I have a fog machine and the kids made a CD of screams. Around the garden I have a scene of crime tape and on the drive a chalk outline of a body!

Leo has chosen his outfit, he will be Eyore from Winnie the Poo! Even I shall be dressing up and playing tricks on the older kids. I am more excited about this than Christmas which is a total non event here anyway.

On Tuesdays I am still working as a volunteer dinner lady serving the food at school with all the bloody Yentas (slang for overbearing Jewish mothers!). They get so stressed out I don't know why they bother as all they do is yell at the kids!

Think Fiddler on the Roof!

This week I was determined to try and keep abreast of current affairs here. So, armed with a stack of ironing I stood for 45 minutes watching a current affairs program with the ex governor of Texas. She did make me laugh, when the interviewer asked her to give her opinion of George Bush in one sentence she said

"Well, how many ways are there to spell stupid"!

Nigel laughed even louder than me when he pointed to the corner of the TV where it said the clip was from May 2002 and was being repeated because that governor had just died! Not that current then. Maybe I'll just stick to watching the Simpsons...

View from Hoo Koo Ee Koo Trail with San Fran in the distance.

November 5th, 2006

HERE COMES THE RAIN AGAIN, FALLING ON MY HEAD LIKE A MEMORY...

Well, how weird was that? I thought the rain had come to stay and I was psyching myself up for six months of nothing but torrential rain, but, it seems to have come and gone again! It is bizarre, last Saturday I burned my back, it was 89 degrees then and yet to-day we went off to a soccer game in shorts and T shirts and Nige had to go back home for jumpers and blankets!

On Wednesday night it started to rain, poor Sam and Ben had to go camping with school. It was hot and sunny the day before they went and the day they returned but in between was like a dam had burst!

This time of year is always the worst for fires; you may have read about 5 firemen being killed out here recently. By the time we get to the end of October there will have been no rain for six months. Everywhere is so dry by then that the fires start easily; the firemen here deserve every penny they get. Sometimes in the mornings we get up and the sky is pink and hazy and you can smell the fires, if it is really bad the kids are kept in during school break times. Despite the recent downfall the trees are glorious in their colours, the mist rolls in until ten am and then it gets up to seventy plus degrees and then the jumpers come off!

This morning was Abbies final soccer game, her team got through to the finals but got beaten to-day 1 -0 after an incredibly close game. I so love going to her games, because all the parents know each other so well after the girls have all played together for a couple of seasons so it is a great social occasion every week. We are now all friends sharing coffees and pastries each Saturday while we yell and scream the kids on. It felt rather sad to realize that this was our last games here.

As I write this Nige has raced off to Santa Rosa, 45 minutes north of here, to take the boys to their game. Abbie and her pals are next door doing homework (allegedly!). It is so nice for her to have a pal next door. Last night the pal was home alone as her parents had gone out so Abbie made some popcorn and ran round in her pajamas to keep her company!

Halloween last week was amazing. We had an open house where anyone and everyone called in for a Bloody Mary and a bite to eat. I had got a great bargain, in the local shop there was a Bat Bar for $150, I waited until the 31st and got it for $38! It's great; it has skulls hanging from the poles and a huge bat with red eyes that light up. Totally naff!

To-day we were all suppose to be swimming with Great White sharks (in a cage!) But, because Abbies' team made it through to the finals we had to cancel so I must reorganise that. What nice parents we are! The dives take place off the Farallon Islands to the West of us where the sharks are studied. Apparently right now is breeding time so you are almost certain to see Jaws! Personally I suspect Nige is trying to cash in on my life insurance, but bugger it, I'll try anything once.

Everything else in life is good, or maybe only until parents evening later this week. It will be so nice to chill out and relax a bit over the winter. Thursday was the first day I spent in my own home for months!

It is a strange feeling to finally settle into a routine here and then realize that this is the last time we will do a lot of things before we move back. I am busy applying for a Return to Nursing Course and Nigel has a couple of interviews lined up. It is so much harder for him as he has just been made a partner in the company here but by the time we leave it will be over a year longer than we originally planned on staying anyway.

Our front garden decorated for Halloween.

The Pumpkin patch, Nicasio

November 27th, 2006

LIFE ON A ROLLERCOASTER

Hello all, I hope this finds you all in the festive spirit. We have just spent a very festive if not somewhat bizarre few days in Los Angeles, but more of that in a jiffy.

Nigel and I were recently invited to a fund raising party by the boob honker! The invitation SHOULD have given me a hint…it was a Leather and Lace party in aid of Marfins Syndrome. When we got there we found that it was $50 each just to get in! Not wishing to look a complete pair of idiots Nige opted to wear his leather motorbike jacket and I wore a T shirt with a bit of lace along the neck line….well, were we totally overdressed or what? There were shaved men in basques, a bride with a rubber dress and Bens teacher, Miss Woody in her full rubber suit. There was hardly enough material amongst them to make a mini-skirt.

Not long after arriving I had my bottom whipped by a man wearing a rubber nappy! Nige refused to drink out of a glass and kept his arse glued to a wall at all times...

It was actually quite a fun evening, there was even a tattoo artist giving free tatts! Part way through the evening the chairwoman got up to tell us about Marfins. Apparently it is a hereditary condition affecting the aorta of those people with exceptionally long limbs and fingers. It is very difficult to detect without extensive tests. All this explained why all night I felt as though I was standing in a hole! Nigel at six feet two was the shortest bloke there!

To cap off an already expensive night there was a silent auction in a private room. To show willing we went in and put $5 over every minimum bid…at the end of the evening we got a bill for several hundred dollars, we had been the only people bidding! I now have a closet full of throws, portraits, hampers, scarves and jewelry!

So, it was an interesting evening but I don't think we are in any hurry to join the local S&M club.

Although the weather has turned chilly by Californian standards and we are still having a bit of rain, I am still out running! Last week-end I took the family on a new running trail that I have recently found. I thought it would be the perfect spot for our annual Christmas photo. It is called Tennessee Valley and is a huge National Park about twenty minutes south of home. The trail takes you over some steep cliffs overlooking the sea along a ridge called Coyote Ridge. As the name suggests this is not somewhere you walk your dog nor is it somewhere you want to find yourself at dusk, which is exactly where we found ourselves after I took us on a wrong turn. Three hours later, just as dark was setting in and my nerve was starting to fail we made it back to the car. That is me, five kids, one of whom was in a backpack, plus a bike. The only person still speaking to me by the time we eventually found the car was the boys' friend Luke who was just grateful that he missed going to Church with his Grandma!

Despite this I have not been put off running the San Fran ½ marathon in February. I just need to reduce the size of the chest Watermelon to do it in relative comfort!

Every now and then I must confess to having doubts about returning to England. We do have a wonderful lifestyle here and six months of annual sunshine is great. Where in the UK can you park your car free of charge, get a beautiful boat ride into a bustling clean city and return home within twenty minutes and be surrounded by mountains and wildlife? Our family time together is so much better here and in one week-end we can travel to snow or sun cheaply.

But, and there always is one, when you continually come up against some truly vile, nasty conceited people which we have had so much of here it restores our conviction to return home. People make places nice to live in, not surroundings.

These last few weeks have been an incredibly emotional time for us all.

A new family has moved into the area with a son the same age as Sam and Ben. This child has spent a lot of time here and the boys have all become good friends. He is now going to the same school as Sam and Ben. I knew the mum from bookclub, and we have even been to their house for dinner recently. On reflection, I now think that this was us being set up for the 'Sting'. This same Mum called me up one day and said she wanted to come over to our house.

Thinking it a social call I put the kettle on and got the chocolate biscuits out. Well, when she arrived she was very hostile and had with her a typed list of truly nasty allegations, one of a sexual nature, against our boys. Rather than be willing to sit down and discuss things rationally she wanted the Police and Lawyers brought in. Needless to say the following week was horrific.

Thankfully, the alleged sexual incidence was witnessed by another adult and his story and that of five other kids collaborated and the new kid admitted to making the allegations up.

The next day at school this same kid got into a fight with another boy where he squeezed this kids neck so hard that his neck had fingerprint bruises on it. The kid asked Sam and Ben and several other boys to go with him to the School Administration to report what had happened but, not before the new kid had phoned his Mum and spun her some more lies. The next thing was that Sam and Ben were hauled up in front of the school Principal and accused of being Gang leaders and bullies!

They were devastated and have not been sleeping well at all and are totally shocked as to why they have been accused of this. As a result, I had to take them out of school for a few days until we could get a meeting arranged with the Principal to find out what the hell was going on. It took a week to get him to speak to us. I had informed the school that I had taken the boys out of school because they were so distressed. The day after our meeting with the school Principal, during which he claimed that the new kid was the one being picked on and the school would be supporting his family, we were sent a letter saying the boys were now classed as truants!! The whole thing has escalated beyond belief. I feel sick to my stomach and I am staggered at the lack of professionalism at that school.

After all that stress it was lovely to escape to Los Angeles for a long weekend. We flew into LAX which takes fifty minutes and spent the next few days in Santa Monica. There, we hired bikes and rollerblades and went right along to Venice beach otherwise known as Muscle Beach. It is all very trendy with lots of shops and street entertainers and frequent filming for videos and commercials. The beach itself is twenty seven miles of pure white sand stretching all the way to Malibu. What the guide books and Hollywood films don't tell you is that it stinks of piss and the amount of homeless people begging is heartbreaking. On the Friday we met up with

Ruby and her family at Disneyland. Now, as many of you may be aware I hate anything that goes up higher than six feet and that turns more than 45 degrees. I suffer these places for the kids and that's it. This particular day was just horrifically busy… or not if you can just put your morals aside for the day...

The friends we went with have Theme parks down to an art; I have to say I laughed and cringed in equal measures and just know that I would not have had the balls to do it myself.

Now, this works only, apparently in Disneyland because it is older and therefore all the entrances are narrower...

So, what our friends do is hire a wheelchair for one of their kids, thus enabling them to go to the front of all the queues for the rides. Plus six guests so there is no waiting at all! Much to my horror this scam works incredibly well. The kids all took turns of being in the wheelchair; the only problem was if they wanted to go on a ride a second time we had to remember which kid had been in the wheelchair the first time round!

OMG, I forgot to mention one of the highlights of our trip! Now I booked this whole trip quite some time ago, when there are six of you traveling I always have everything planned in detail. You can, therefore, imagine my horror of finding out that the car I had hired to collect at the airport had been given to someone else and, on a national holiday week-end there were no other hire companies that had cars left big enough for all of us. To say I spat my dummy out at the hire company is an understatement! After an hour I eventually found a very sweet Indian guy willing to loan us an 8 seater car. The said car was a 15 year old bottle green Chevrolet. Now, you know when you rent a car you do the walk round inspection to note any nicks and scrapes? Well, this car had a boulder dent for every one of its 15 years of life. All the interior vinyl was split and Leo's car seat had a bit of towel for a cover. The best part was when we arrived at Disneyland and parked the car.

When we all got out I could still hear the engine going so asked Nige to turn it off. He looked at me and held up his hand, he had taken the key out the ignition but the engine was still going! The kids nicknamed it 'The Crapster'!

You can imagine the look on the faces of both Nige and the valet parking guys at THE Beverly Hills Hotel when we pulled up in this car!! I was peeing myself laughing inside but managed to keep a straight face, patted the valet on the shoulder and asked him to look after my Limo!

I swear to God you have never seen anything like it.

As for the hotel, well it is everything you can possibly imagine.

Absolutely stunning, the staff were so nice and friendly. The suite made me want to cry, there were welcome letters for each of the kids, teddies in the bed, bath toys and warm cookies. They all got a free soft drinks 'debit' card for all the bars and cafes. We checked in on Saturday and spent the afternoon exploring the grounds and hanging out by the pool.

The hotel is set in twelve acres of beautiful lush gardens. To walk around the bungalows where Marilyn Monroe and Liz Taylor stayed and hang out by the pool that you have seen in Hello magazine was just fab.

The pool even has private cabanas around it where you can entertain guests or have massages.

Kids being kids immediately set up a rapport with all the staff and they all fell in love with Leo the Lion who was as charming as always!

On Saturday morning we wandered around a guaranteed celebrity spotting place….the Hollywood Forever Cemetery where you can buy a map to find the graves of some of Hollywoods' greatest

Charlie Chaplin

Jayne Mansfield

Cecil B De Mille

Rudolph Valentino

to name a few.

We also had a drive out to Malibu, though I have to say we found it really disappointing. The road out is really badly maintained with cramped housing along the sea front. The houses are really narrow and squashed so tightly together that there is no room for parking, if you farted in one house they'd hear it three doors down! On one side is the housing and on the other just barren hills interspersed with a few malls and restaurants. Nothing special at all, just another case of hyping up the Hollywood fantasy. Personally I think LA is great for a visit but for the most part it is just a huge flat mass of industry (it is the biggest port in the US). The rich and famous bit we all think of is tiny, probably five square miles within a triangle of three streets. Santa Monica Blvd., Sunset Blvd and Rodeo Drive. This is where the celebs live, work and play. Hardly any wonder that they have no idea of life outside the bubble.

On Saturday afternoon we hung around the hotel and then had lunch at the Farmers Market opposite CBS studios. Within fifteen minutes of sitting down at one of the wonderful outdoor cafes we had been approached by an agent asking us to take the three older kids along to audition the following day! It is plain to see how easy it would be to get suckered into this would be luvvie environment. That night we went for dinner at The Grove, this is a huge shopping Mall that is designed to look like a European street. It was wonderful, huge Christmas trees and even fake snow falling, which was very weird as we were walking round in shorts and T shirts!

On Sunday morning we had brunch in the Polo Lounge. It was every bit as glamorous as you would imagine. I had gone to sit at a table while I waited for Nige and the kids to arrive. The waiter came over and asked me if I would like a glass of Champagne. Naturally I did not refuse, well, every time he walked past me he topped my glass up. When Nige did arrive he looked at the menu. He asked me if I was enjoying the champers, when I said yes it was delicious he said good because according to the menu it was $62 a glass!!! It was a very expensive brunch.

That afternoon we went window shopping along Rodeo drive, the kids saw some kid from the Suite Life of Zac and Cody but that was it as far as celebrity spotting.

We flew back home late Sunday night. I must say I shall miss week-ends like this.

Hanging out at the pool at The Beverly Hills Hotel.

Christmas on Rodeo Drive

December 21st, 2006

JUST ANOTHER DECEMBER

Well it is official, the month of December has been cancelled in the Barrett house!

Almost every year we have some kind of crisis and this year we have had a job lot!

We started the month on a good note. We had Nigels 40th birthday bash and took 16 friends out for a slap up meal in his fave restaurant and yes, surprise, surprise we ended up in the Silver friggin' Peso drinking Tequilas until some hideous hour!

Come to think of, maybe that's when the bad luck started because we left our table flower arrangement there and when I went back for it not a soul knew anything about it...

That was the good part of the month. The week after that we ended up with a bloody lawyer like true f***ing Californians. Lets' not discuss our problems, lets' pay someone else to sought it out for us. This was all relating to that dreadful situation with the boys I mentioned a while ago. There have been lots of tears and anxiety and we are now several thousand dollars poorer too. We ended up having a meeting between the school principal, the district supervisor and our lawyer acting as a mediator. It went in our favour in the end. The Principal behaved appallingly and walked out of the meeting. Not before he had to agree to make a formal apology to our boys for the dreadful wrongful accusations he made against them. I have had to get all past school reports and speak to all of their previous teachers to prove he was wrong and all because of this vile family. The Principal had tried to say that the boys had come from the junior school with a 'stack' of self- management cards and disciplinary reports. There was no truth to this at all as proved. Sam got that one self management card for running in the library. All their school reports were lovely and complimentary and they had received no kind of disciplinary at all. I have since found out that the kid who caused all the problems has been to several different schools and caused the same sort of problems at each. Maybe the school Principal should have found this out for himself before he started making false accusations! The only reason

I can think of for the reason the mother started all this is because she is currently being investigated for giving illegal drugs to her patients. Maybe she was looking to sue us to pay for her own legal costs at being caught out by the feds!

I am disgusted at what we have had to go through, especially our poor boys who are just bewildered by it all. They are now scared of going into school and don't trust the teachers.

It has really made us sit up and think about our lives and what we want to do with them. Obviously, the first thing it has made us want to do is run from here as soon as possible. Sadly, despite all the wonderful experiences we have had here this has left a lasting nasty taste.

It would break my heart to think that England will ever get like it is here although the more we read and hear the more likely that seems to be the case. We were reading about the Hertfordshire boy with the exemplary school record who shoved the school bully and was subsequently charged by the police?

Well, that is so like here and is so not what we want for our children. It made us think about all the things that make your life good, like customs and traditions, being able to say Happy Christmas and not offend someone by saying it. I am sure the average Joe Bloggs on the street has no problem respecting other peoples cultures and beliefs. It's the petty government gone PC mad.

For our Jewish friends we wish them Happy Hanukkah, our black friends Happy Kwanza. Whatever your faith or belief we wish you well. We have been to Jewish festivals, celebrated Hanukkah and Kwanza and enjoyed it all and yet we are scowled at for saying Happy Christmas. This has led us to think that, just maybe we would like to move away from the Bush and Blair puppet shows to somewhere we can say these things and where our taxes don't go to fighting a different war every few years, where education is good and decent healthcare is available for all.

All this, at first, led us to think of New Zealand until Nigel pointed out that North Africa and New Zealand are about the only places he has no chances of getting a job!

I digress, as for the rest of the month. The week after Nigels birthday I was driving near our house when the car in front of me hit the central reservation and flipped over 360degrees and landed on its roof. I was on my knees trying to get the people out through the window as smoke and petrol poured out and the ignition was still on. Thank goodness there was only one young lad of seventeen and he was shocked but OK. He told me this was his THIRD car, but that his uncle, who ran a BMW garage would get him another one. What were his parents thinking of? Plus, his friend arrived and I heard them admit that they were racing each other. Bloody idiots.

My birthday on the 18th was nice. Nige took me out for dinner and then to the movies to see the new Bond film, Casino Royale. I have to say that Nige is the connoisseur of Bond men and even he thought Daniel Craig was pretty good. Not bad for a Chester lad! Praise indeed.

Nigels work Christmas do was another thing altogether with me missing it due to a bout of dodgy tummy syndrome.

Then, if things were not bad enough Nigels' parents arrived after a trip around the world only for his Dad to suffer a minor stroke in the early hours of the following morning. He is now in the local hospital receiving excellent treatment and care courtesy of having full travel insurance!

The up side is that it happened whist they were here with us and not alone in the back of beyond. We are hoping they let him out for Christmas if not we'll have it in the hospital!

I wonder what else can possibly go wrong?

LIVING WITH THE BUNNIES
A BRITISH FAMILYS' EXILE TO MARIN COUNTY.

YEAR FOUR

Contents

January 19th, 2007

SINCE LAST TIME

I'm bored, I hate this time of year. There's nothing to look forward to and the weather is freezing. I know I shouldn't moan, I really do, but I always feel miserable at this time of year. I use to think I had that weird condition where you don't get enough sunlight but I've lived here for three years now and I am still a miserable cow in January so that blows that theory then!

Since I last wrote Nigel's Dad has made a fantastic recovery from his stroke and has been able to return home to the UK. Thankfully the stroke occurred in a minor blood vessel so the after effects were short lasting and did no major damage.

Ultimately he is 77 years old, was eleven months post by-pass and a trip around the world was just too much for him.

The kids all went back to school on the 9th of this month which was just too long a holiday by my books! They were ready to kill each other and I was ready to kill Sam as he left his new bike at school on the last Friday of school and by the Monday it had been nicked! This is, I have to say, pretty unusual around here. It is still the kind of area where no-one locks their front door and they leave the keys in the ignition.

At our house there is no lock on the bloody door anyway!

The weather, so far, has been amazing. After the dreadful rain we had this time last year we have had beautiful clear skies and warm sunshine in the afternoons. It has been frosty on a few mornings but by 10am it has gone and then it has been jeans and T shirt weather!

That, however, was not the case this week-end. On Friday night we drove south east of here to a place called Modesto for a Football Tournament for the boys. We left Abbie at a friends house as she had yet another Bar Mitzvah to attend.

So, we booked into a cheap and cheerful hotel with the rest of the soccer team. In front of our room was the equivalent of the M1 and immediately behind us the equivalent of the Euston line. The giveaway should have been when the receptionist gave us all a set of earplugs when we checked in…

The 'piece de resistance' was the 'shagging for the Olympics' couple in the room next to us.

I was SO tired that I was an utter bitch by Sunday lunchtime.

Add onto this that Saturdays first game was at 8am and the pitch was a 45 minute drive away and the coach wanted them there by 7:30am, the shaggers didn't stop until 4:30am and Sam and Ben had set the alarm for 5am instead of 6am!

To add insult to injury they lost on a penalty shootout!

On Jan 6th we were invited to the annual traveling street party where you have cocktails in one house, dinner in the next and dessert in the following one and coffee in the last. It was really quite fun to meet all the neighbours. I fell in love with an 85 year old Italian man who, up until a few years ago, still biked across Europe with a tent on his back! He was really interesting and has promised to cook us some fine Italian cuisine! We also met a guy who has had a book published this month called The Luck of the Shamen.

Coffee was at our immediate neighbours who is the retired Crown Judge of California appointed by Ronnie Reagan who was also a personal friend of his.

This explains the truly enormous American Flag outside his house! Apparently, he was telling us, that during high profile court cases that our road would be protected by Armed Guards for his personal safety!

Remember I mentioned that living here could sometimes feel like a Police State?

Well, get this, I found out this week that there is a curfew in each local town ranging from 10pm to 11pm. If your 17 / 18 year old is caught outside after this time then the parents can be fined! So, they are old enough to get married, fight in Iraq but cannot go to the movies in their home town!

The best one of the week goes to the control freak of a school principal at the kids' school who announced over the loud speaker system that if anyone wore shorts to school then they would get a detention. What the hell has it got to do with him? There is no uniform policy at the school! Talk about a power ego trip, this man wins the prick of the century award! The pettiness of this place drives me insane, it's because of people like him that nutters go into schools and shoot kids and why fifteen year olds throw themselves off the Golden Gate Bridge. Speaking of which, some weirdo has made a docufilm about the suicides off the bridge called The Bridge. A film crew spent every night for a year on the bridge filming people jumping off. They managed to save six but there were thirty four attempted suicides altogether. The city bigwigs are now in the process of putting up a fence to stop people being able to climb up onto the railings to jump...

This coming week-end Nigel and the boys are off to the State capital of Sacramento for the State Cup final. I alas, have been relegated to chauffeur duty for Abbies busy social life. Tonight it is the monthly Rec. dance for all the local schools and tomorrow is an ice skating party. I cannot believe my week-ends are spent shaving my daughters legs for her and giving her advice like "if a boy tries to kiss you tell him you have a throat infection and if he puts his hands on your bum during the 'slowies' shout,

"Your hands are on my ass so move them now"!

Oh, the joys of parenting!

February 14th, 2007

SITTING ON THE DOCK OF THE BAY WATCHING TIME DRIFT AWAY

The weeks really do fly as you get older don't they? We have had a month full of the usual frantic school / sport and general taxi servicing that we provide free of charge, except for the odd kiss and hug, for our kids!

Sam and Bens' soccer season came to an end after seven long months, and we hosted the end of season party…as is becoming a very boozy routine. We had sixteen kids and blah parents. There were trophies and certificates galore and one Dad who is a whiz on the computer and camera front made a fab CD and a lovely photo for each child. As has become the norm the party is suggested as being from 5-7pm and the die hards stagger home at midnight! These past few weeks have seen Abbie get an 'All American' brace, for that read fookin' posh parents who all want their kids to look like a Colgate advert. I had to sit down when they told me it will cost $6,545..times that by four and we are seriously considering at least three of them go up for adoption..

Two weeks ago I had my very own 'I'm about to hit forty' but I want to be tasteful crisis. So, Nige gets the Death Machine that only gets wheeled out the garage if there is no rain forecast and the temperature is guaranteed to be at least 70 degrees...and I get a tattoo!

After hours of sober deliberation I decide on a personalized small tattoo on the base of my back. Four circles interlinked (to represent my four darlings) into a Gaelic knot. I was sober because

a) It was 9:30 am and

b) The woman on the desk had a body and face dedicated to science for the purpose of tolerance to pain and self abuse and scared the crap out of me!

How exactly I managed to come out then with a tattoo and my nose pierced is not quite clear yet...

I was feeling really quite proud of myself until Jenn came round and she said,

"Wow Fi, you got your very own Tramp stamp".

She is now my ex friend!

Nigel on the other hand thought it was very sexy, or will be when the scabs have fully healed, and is now considering having the abbreviated form of Welcome to Barbados on his didgery doo…

In keeping with the whole hippie thing last week we went off to the city to visit the Ashbury / Haight district where the Hippie movement first started. It was full of very colouful characters and body piecing establishments. Been there, done that, and have definitely not crossed the line into some pain loving sub culture!

We spent a lovely afternoon wandering around the shops and found a really great Indian restaurant for Sunday dinner! Nige knows the area quite well as it is Rugby season once again and so every Saturday morning, at some hideous hour, he slinks off down the Haight to find a pub sad enough to show the crucifixion of the Welsh rugby team on a weekly basis. See, Nige is really into the S&M scene and so goes back every week...

This week we went to see Abs in her school production of the Wizard of Oz. I was given very specific instructions as to seating location, laughter levels and audience participation. As a result I sat tied and gagged at the very back of the hall. I must say she did a fab job as the evil witch of the East, infact very little acting or dressing up required…bless.

On the job front, I have now put on the calendar that the 1st of May is the official day of when it is OK for me to panic. Up until this date 'something' will come up and all will be fine. After then of course we are looking to be

a) homeless

b) jobless

c) countryless

So, all great until then.

Thus far Nige has had a job offer, over nine interviews between here, New York and London only to find that the person advertising the 'new job' has been fired!

Like I said, all is well until May 1st.

March 11th, 2007

JET LAGGED AGAIN!

Well, its 5am, the washing machine is on, the kids are bouncing around, I've just had lunch, dinner or was it breakfast?

We arrived back here yesterday afternoon after an eleven hour bumpy flight which was a tad scary at the end as when we were coming in to land we had another plane so close to us that we could see the pilots face! However, this flight was better than the one going out to the UK which took twelve and a half hours as it was so windy at Heathrow the pilot could not land the plane. After several attempts we ran out of fuel, diverted to Gatwick to re-fuel and then back to Heathrow to try again. Hideous, it was like a fairground ride.

We had a lovely few days in Chester, a wonderful night out on the Saturday and then a seven hour drive back to London thanks to the driver not having a clue where the Dorchester Hotel is. He was using a Satnav to get us there, I had assumed he had put in Park Lane as the address but no, he had put in only Dorchester. We drove down every road, café, brothel and B&B before I asked him what address he had typed in! The two of us were ready to commit infacide four times over because of the kids' whinging and squabbling. Nigel called from the hotel to say all the staff were waiting to greet us as they were excited at having kids come to stay as there hadn't been any for a while…the driver and I just looked at each other and started laughing!

The hotel was gorgeous when we eventually found it! It is owned by the same chain that owns the Beverly Hills Hotel and is very similar. It might be expensive to stay there but they don't even have tea and coffee making facilities in the rooms! When I phoned down for a cuppa tea it was £15! I drank a lot of water that week. Needless to say we only ate there once!

We hired a car for two days and spent them clearing out the loft and shed of our old house, Magnolia Cottage, and doing runs to the tip, charity shops and to a storage unit. We did laugh as what to do with one particular box that was full of Ann Summers vibrators from when I used to work for them before we were married. I still remember all the names too, the Black Prince, the Greek Adonis…

In true chav style I had a load of washing to do. Now the Dorchester charges £12 to wash your socks so I put all the washing in a posh Hotel bag and lugged it to HemelHempsted and into the nearest launderette! £6 for the lot. Bargain!

We spent the Monday at the Embassy standing in queues, filling in forms and hanging round a lot waiting for our visas to be renewed.

By Friday morning the cold I had from the Sunday and which had got progressively worse meant the Hotel Doctor had to be called for. I was diagnosed with Bronchitis and plonked on anti-biotics and Ventolin inhalers. It was the first time I have been poorly in three years and I felt right proper sorry for myself!

Nigel did have yet more interviews for the London job so things are looking quite promising there. We just have to wait and see what the salary offer will be. Then we have to make the big decision of whether we want to live in central London or hold out here and wait for something else to come up. In the meantime I am looking for yet another Return to Nursing Course as the second one I got a place on has had the funding withdrawn.

I thought England was crying out for Nurses?

March 27th, 2007

THREE YEARS ON

Well, last Friday marked the third anniversary of our being here. Instead of fondly reflecting on our time here we seem to be engrossed in our efforts to leave! This job offer for Nige has still not been put in writing but he is suppose to be meeting with some lawyers to discuss the visa issue. This is our biggest concern as in his line of work if his current employer gets wind of him applying elsewhere then they will literally escort him from the building there and then. As his boss is our sponsor to be here in America then as soon as Nige leaves his job then our visa is null and void. We would then have 28 days to leave the country. Bit stressful!

I have found yet another return to nursing course, this one in Buckinghamshire.

This one is a self funded one so hopefully this means the Health Authority cannot cancel it. If all goes well then that just leaves the logistics of where we live. It is this one that is causing the most anguish. The most positive thing to come out of our time here has been in the improvement of our family time. Nige works flexi(ish) hours, plus has a short commute to work that is virtually free. This has meant that for the first time he has been able to attend parent evenings and school concerts and the like which has meant a huge amount to the kids. To do this in England we would have to live in central London because of the hours he would work and that just won't work for me. Decisions, Decisions!

As for here, the weather is warming up nicely. This weekend we had a BBQ for friends. We spent last week with our Jewish friends celebrating St Patricks Day!

Next week we have little Leo's birthday party. I am stunned that he will be four soon! We are having a party at home with a magician and he is so excited! Where did those four years go?

Abbie still seems to have a Bar Mitzvah party most week-ends, her social life is better than mine ever was! I have to confess to being Miss Millie Tant again this week, fuck, that school hates me! We received a snotty letter saying that Abbie had still not completed all the tests, work, quizzes etc that she missed whilst we were away in England. I tried to point out that she had done a detailed diary, completed the necessary work books and read two books and visited numerous classic museums AND that despite awful jet lag they had all arrived in school the day after arriving back here and that they were all doing their best to cope with an incredible workload plus trying to catch up on missed work. I also felt compelled to point out that Marin County has one of the highest teenage suicide rates in the US and that was maybe due to the pressure to perform that is put on kids here! They just don't get it here, it does not occur to them that kids might travel out of America and suffer things like Jetlag, all they see are performance figures and the need to pacify the Pushy Parent Brigade! These are the parents who want to ensure that 'precious' gets into one of the Ivy League schools before the poor kid is out of nappies! If I speak to the teachers individually then they agree it is it ridiculous but the school administration is terrified of the litigacious parents here. I gave up doing the lunch bar / dinner lady duties because of all the overprotective Yenta mothers. They are all just so stressed and aggressive!

Last week I was horrified to be sent an email accusing me of sending racist jokes about the Irish. This was from someone I considered a good friend (Lena, my jogging partner) and whom I thought had a sense of humour.

Evidently not! Imagine if I got the hump everytime you lot sent me a joke about Scousers! It just went to show that you cannot tell with people here, I have now stopped sending any kind of jokes to people here. They all look for reasons to be offended, probably hoping to get a lawsuit out of it! How sad is that?

Then you get talking to a local who just fails to believe that you don't simply totally adore everything about Marin County.

Maybe it is me who is the victim of racism here?

On a lighter note, the Spring Soccer season has started, much to the kids delight. Especially Sam and Ben as we had to let their places on the Select team go as we could not commit to being here for another year. They have been really upset but have tried to be incredibly mature about it all, bless them!

Anyway, it is late and I want to get to my book. This month it is called The Devils Teeth and is about work done by Marine biologists on the Farallon Islands to the West of here and about their work with the Great White sharks that inhabit the sea around there. Scary to say the least, guaranteed to have your ten year old nose deep in a book! Another great book I read recently was called May Contain Nuts by a British author whose name eludes me now. It is about the lengths parents will go to in order to get their kids into a school of their choice. It made me cringe for criticizing the Marinites!

The book is so funny that Nige hid it from me to stop me laughing aloud in bed when he is trying to sleep!

April 11th, 2007

WHAT COMES AROUND GOES AROUND

Happy Easter to you all. I hope you had a good one. Our kids have been off for the week. On Friday we were at Jenns' house to help stuff 1200 plastic eggs with sweets for their annual Easter Egg hunt in a local park. She plied us with food and wine which just about took the edge off the frustration of trying to find two halves of eggs that would match up! Nige went off to the park at some hideous hour on the Sunday to be the Easter bunny and hide the 1200 eggs. It is a great day, everyone brings food, there are two hunts, one for the older kids and one for the under fives. There is a Golden Egg with a $20 bill in to encourage the older ones to join in. All in all there are over a hundred people there. After the food and hunt we play games with raw eggs, we all end up pretty messy! This year the weather was just gorgeous as it has been for the last few weeks, about 80 degrees.

On Saturday we had Leos' fourth birthday party with a magician who pulled real birds out of a hat. He took being the 'assistant' very seriously in his Superman outfit!

The kids left early but the hardened party girls were still here at 10pm. We were all sat on our bed with the door locked and lots of wine and gossiped. I just love girlfriends!

The beginning of our week was not so great and we are hoping that bad luck does not travel in threes. On the Thursday night it was Abbies' soccer training and I had six kids with me. The boys were all off to one side playing soccer and I was playing with Leo and watching Abbie. I then heard Ben shout that Sam had been hurt. I turned around and Sam is on his knees holding his head and there is blood running between his fingers and onto the ground. The silly buggers had been throwing rocks at a target, Sam had bent down to fasten his shoelace when a rock bounced off the curb and hit him on the head. It cut a gash across his scalp, I had to try and get him and the other five in the car and race to the hospital where he had it stitched together. To see the amount of blood it looked like the chainsaw massacre! He was really brave; it was poor Ben that was the wreck! Thankfully, it was on his hairline so unless he develops a receding hairline then no-one will ever know.

On the Sunday afternoon we had been to a friends house for a BBQ, a really nice new English family who have been living in France for the last five years and have moved here to look after the Dads parents who live in San Fran. Their kids are so lucky, Dad is German, so they speak that fluently and because of living in France they are also fluent in French so all in all at the ages of 8 and 11 they are trilingual.

So, after spending a lovely day with them Nige, Leo and I went for a walk with Raffy in our neighbourhood. We had not got to the end of our road when I heard a shout and looked up to see this woman with a German Shepherd on a lead and a Boxer running straight at us. In seconds it was on us and grabbed Raffy by the head and threw him against a wall trying to get to his belly and biting into his head and neck in an absolute frenzy. The next moment the woman has lost control of the German Shepherd as well. I was knocked over but managed to pull Leo up and out of the frenzy, he was hysterical as you can imagine. I ran to the nearest house and banged on the door to get him to safety. In the meantime Nigel was fighting off these dogs trying to get to Raffy. Someone must have called the police and there was a very ugly scene between me and the dogs' owner. She took no responsibility at all, she asked Nigel to tell me not to yell at her! In true Marin style she played the victim and even asked if Leo would like to stroke the dogs who she said were lovely and wouldn't have attacked him! That makes ripping my dog to shreds ok then????

We rushed Raffy to the vets for bites to his neck. He was in a right state. The police here will not get involved and refer dog attacks to the equivalent of the RSPCA. I am pushing for a hearing to have her dogs registered as dangerous but my chances are slim. After all we live in an environment where there are dog hotels, dog bakeries, clothes shops for dogs; you can take them into Department stores but, oh, don't let them off a lead, ever! When I phoned the owner up to ask if she was willing to pay the vets bills I told her I thought that her dogs were a danger to the community as they live on a narrow road leading into the school grounds, and that I was prepared to take the matter further. To this she told me to 'bring it on' as she was an attorney and would beat me hands down.

That just about sums up the people of Marin for me and yet the Americans wonder why the rest of the world hates them. Well, you do not have to look too far around here to see why.

There has been another school fundraiser to hit that $1 million mark. This one is called Tombola. It was $125 per person just to attend (we did not go...) and was held in a warehouse in San Fran. A coach was provided to ferry the parents there and back. Everyone had to go dressed up as a popstar or movie star. The whole night is about bidding ridiculous amounts of money on an auction. The food and wine is provided and the idea is to get you hopelessly drunk so that you part with your money. The money spent blows your mind. Someone paid $4,500 for their ten year old to be school Principal for the day. Exotic holidays went for $20,000, all this money and some parents puked up on the coach coming home. Classic!

For the last three days we have been staying at Ruby Tuesday's cabin on the Russian river. It was just beautiful. We took a pal for Abbie and all the kids spent their time kayaking in the river which is literally at the bottom of the garden. Leo spent almost the entire time in their hot tub on the patio! I embedded myself on a garden hammock with a book and Nigel cooked BBQ's.

Nigels'current boss, in the past few months, has started to behave very oddly. Now, we are talking about a man who went on a golfing holiday, arrived at his destination airport to have the cab driver open the boot to put his luggage in. Only at this point did he realize that he had only the clothes he was standing in. He had assumed that someone else had packed for him! Every Monday morning it is his secretary's job to go around the city and try to find where he has left his car after going out drinking the Friday night before! He desperately wants to be anything but American, and who can blame him? He tries to live as a Frenchman, even insisting his kids are educated at a French school! It would seem that he has become bored with being a multi millionaire (isn't life a bitch?) and has decided to spice things up a little. He has come to the conclusion that an autocratic leadership style is the way forward (did someone mutter Thatcher?)

He has taken to asking the people who work for him if they are stupid. Nice. He has also taken to hiring and firing people Willy nilly. He has now employed a dreadful Japanese woman to 'handle' the investment fund managers who has no prior experience at all. She has been in a firing frenzy (his boss is too spineless to do it himself). Nige says that the atmosphere in the office is just awful; no-one has lunch together any more. The crunch came this week when they interviewed for an assistant for Nigel. They just didn't tell him or involve him in any way. This has been a turning point for us really. There is no way Nige wants to continue working in this environment and there is no way we even want to consider getting a mortgage here with a boss likely to fire you for wearing the wrong colour tie to the office!

So, it seems 99% likely that at the end of the school year (June 24th) we shall be heading home. I am busy looking at houses in Buckinghamshire where it would be easy for Nige to commute and me to do the Return To Nurse Practice Course.

Here we go!

May 7th, 2007

PONYTAILED AND PRIVILIDGED

Well, the May 1st deadline headed 'to-day Fiona can panic' has passed and I am still doing remarkably well all things considered! Like having to move 6,000 miles in seven weeks and having no home to live in or in fact no real idea what area we are going to live in! After taking a year to go through the whole interview process with the new job they have all of a sudden got a rocket up their arse and are on countdown to launch! We got an email on Thursday requesting that Nigel resign the following day! At this point Nige did confess to me that he had told the new company that we were moving back to the UK anyway so therefore they will not pay our moving expenses.. and also that we had kept a house there that we could move back into! They of course believe then that this is a nice uncomplicated easy move. I was not impressed!

So, we stalled them until the Monday when he had to resign as we had now run out of ideas as how to stall them any further. I was very proud of him as he was very honest to his current boss and told him the reason he was leaving was because he had become too erratic and unpredictable to work for any longer. He had two days off and then started working for the new company! They have a small office in San Fran which is where the company first started during the gold Rush era of the 1840's. So far he has spent 4 days in New York and next week he will be in London and then onto Japan! He was squirming about meeting the 'big boys' as an ex employee has written a kiss and tell book about working for Lennards, and it is not pretty reading! We were trying out various scenarios as to what he should say if anyone asks whether he has read the book or not!

Last Sunday we had a Yard Sale to sell off all of our plants and electrical goods. It went really well so we are planning another one at the end of June to sell off the remaining lamps, TV's and the like. We think we will leave here on the 24th of June and then bugger off to the Bahamas for a week before heading back home.

We are all feeling a bit weird at times. I felt particularly bad last week as the boys received a letter asking them to try out for the

Soccer Junior Olympic team which is pretty fantastic. Yesterday they all had their last matches of the spring Soccer league and so now they know that this is the end of their soccer life here although they will continue to train with their 'select' soccer team right up until we go.

The game yesterday was really awkward, Nigel was coaching the team and their opponents had the kid that made all the dreadful allegations last December so it was a very personal game for Sam and Ben. We told them to play hard but fair and to behave like gentlemen at all costs. What I really wanted to say to them was to annihilate the little fucker! It was a fast and hard game, Abbie played with them to support them. We called her 'The Rash' because she was all over the field! They were two all when the little fucker himself headed one into the back of the net as the whistle blew. I could have cried for them but the boys were stars and went over and shook hands and said well done. I was very proud of them, poor Nigel kept waking up last night reliving it all and getting more and more cross! It was not the best way to end their games here but a good learning experience in life and they were very gracious.

That whole situation has a lasting legacy, Sam still has nightmares now. As for the school, well the formal apology for Sam never came. Just on Friday I had to go to the school office and the Principals wife was there, she gave me the filthiest look possible. I just thought how totally unprofessional they both are. It is very much an establishment where the head likes to be in total control and does not like to be questioned at all. The parents don't like to question the administration for fear of negative repercussions on their kids so it is really reinforced bullying. I shall be so glad to leave the petty politics of this area where it is all formal pleasantries and totally insincere. The mothers all wear their trendy jogging suits with the pony tail swinging and the coffee in the hand smiling the perfect $500 white smile and swan off to lunch in their big SUV's whilst the Mexican nannies take care of their kids and someone else does the cleaning and gardening. It is so much a culture of paying someone else to do everything for them so they can absolve themselves of any responsibility or accountability.

Speaking of which, we have received a letter asking us to a 'mediation' meeting with the owners of the dogs that attacked Rafferty. What's that all about then? Are we going to compare food brands and talk about the best local doggie hotels? Or which doggie bakery makes the best organic dog cookies? Purleese, give me a break! I really don't think I can trust myself to go along and listen to the crap they will try and feed us. Maybe they will suggest that Raffy goes into therapy to find out just what it was in his psyche that made those lovely dogs just want to rip him to pieces. Maybe it will all turn out that he was the youngest of the litter and just never got over it.... maybe he is a female in a males body and maybe it is all just a load of absolute bollocks!

A couple of week-ends ago we went off exploring a place in San Fran called the Sutro Baths. These were pools carved into the cliffs which then filled with tidal sea water. They were the play area of the cities wealthiest residents in the mid 1800's. There were some pools inside and varied in temperature. Altogether they held 24,000 people! There was a hotel resort called The Cliff House which had a museum and restaurants. The House had burned down three times, the replica building there now has a fab seafood restaurant that overlooks a huge rock full of wild cormorants and brown pelicans and some very vocal sea lions! Alongside the restaurant are five miles of sand beaches called Ocean Beach. Contrary to what you might imagine much of Californias' beaches are not safe to swim at all. The beach was virtually empty so we spent hours playing soccer and building sandcastles. All the baths are pretty much gone now but you can walk among the ruins and imagine what it was like back then. There is a wonderful manmade tunnel that has a hole halfway through where the sea thunders in and assumedly use to fill the pools. The other end opened onto rugged rocks and the sight was fantastic as the waves crashed over them making rainbows against the sun. I could have stood for hours watching that.

We ended the day wandering around a suburb called Cow Hollow where we found a little tea shop and we gorged ourselves on warm bread and strawberry jam.

Yum!

We are having a heatwave at the moment; it was 95 yesterday and 79 by 8:30am this morning and due to be even hotter later on. Yesterday we found a lovely beach in Sausalito where the kids can swim in the Bay. For once you can take dogs on the sand but it was too hot for poor Raffy so the kids hired kayaks and Raffy and I sat in the shade watching them having fun.

On Friday we had Abbies' track meet which is a huge Sports day for all the local schools. The kids have to try out to take part and have training three times a week for a few weeks beforehand. They compete on a full size track with a proper starter gun and have field events too. It is all very serious indeed! I had to laugh at all the over competitive parents screaming at their kids and often running the track with them before the races. Everyone pretends to be really cool but there is a definite undercurrent of serious competitiveness. Bearing in mind this is a culture of helicopter parenting and child idolization,

"Well done darling, awesome blinking and breathing darling!"

Abbie was chosen to run the 600 metres and the high jump. She did really well and will now go on to the County Track meet to compete against the fastest ones of this meet. She does make me laugh, she is like a Gazelle now and will be taller than me by her birthday, and yes I do know that's not particularly hard!

On Friday night I went to see Hot Fuzz, the movie. It was really funny because the woman who runs the cinema asked if there were any Brits in the audience. Four of us raised our hands and she told everyone else that we would be the only ones that would understand the humour and that the rest of the audience should try not to be offended by it!!

Ocean Beach, San Francisco.

May 28th, 2007

LAST BUT ONE

I suspect that this will be the last but one newsletter before we head home. What a strange feeling that is too. We are busy trying to cram in all the mini trips we have been meaning to do and re-visit our favourite places for a last time. Things are slowly coming together, we now have a house to move into and have sent off application forms for the kids to start school in September. The boys will go to an all boys' school and Abbie will probably go privately as there are no places left at the school we would like her to go to until next year. The three of them are remarkably fine with the whole single sex school thing. Obviously the raging hormones have not kicked in yet! We have rented a house in Cookham in Berkshire, I saw it online and Nigels' parents have been to have a look at it for us.

It seems an odd idea to move into a house you have never seen but we have done it before!

So, we are going to be a bit nomadic for a month first and probably be a bit smelly too. We move out of this house on June 26th into a hotel, then on the 29th we fly to Miami and on the 30th we felt we deserved a holiday in the Bahamas! The islands are only an hour from Miami and then a little seaplane to our tiny island of Columbus where it is Club Med all the way! Nothing to do but eat, drink read and snorkel. Perfecto!

After ten days of serious relaxation we fly back to Miami for a few days and then into London to the Mayfair Hotel for a week before moving into the new house!

So, we will basically have the same clothes from June 26th until July 18th.

We are all quite excited now. We are having a leaving party on the 7th which will be nice. To be honest there are very few people we will miss but the good friends we have made here are great and have saved my sanity on many occasions. Who knows, I may end up doing a newsletter to them about what it's like to be back in England!

Last week-end we went to see a show with Bens' ex teacher in, Miss Woody? It was her debut show in a tiny theatre in the city. It was totally not what I expected, it was a show about her life, she was sexually abused by her brother from aged 7.

The show was about how she has accepted what happened to her and has used the experience to make herself stronger. It was really quite 'dark' in places but with a touch of humour too. It really was brilliantly done. She is about to embark on a National tour with the show, it takes guts to do that. She got totally humiliated by that awful school, and yet re-mortgaged her house and took out loans to follow her dream. Good for her, she's ace. In her words, she is a kickass gal!

So, seven of us went out for the night, we had lots of wine during the show, Mel had set up a bar in a little room off the theatre and then afterwards we followed our noses and found an Indian restaurant round the corner. After we sat down we realized the restaurant had no license so three of us went off looking for an Off License to buy beer and a corkscrew!

To-day is Sam and Bens 11th birthday! We made a week-end of it and had a really lovely time. On Friday we went away to a place called Healdsburg which is about an hour and a half drive north of here into the wine Country. It is a very smart colonial type town with a beautiful park in the middle and then grand shops all round the edge. There were lots of boutique type shops as well as Ralph Lauren furniture shops. We managed to find a wonderful old fashioned sweet shop decked out as Willy Wonkers Chocolate Factory which was owned by an English man so he had English sweets like Curlie Wurlies and Maltesers. We spent a fair amount of money in there!

Whilst we were there it was 'Fayre Day' where there were lots of stalls, a mini circus and an animal auction. As well as being a very prosperous town it is also a real farming town. Each year the farmers give their kids an animal to rear for a year and fatten up and then they sell the animal at auction for slaughter. They make quite a bit of money to put towards a college fund. Apparently if you have a 200lbs pig they can earn $7 a pound from it. They very proudly told us all about rearing these pigs, goats and sheep. Of course there was the pet dog competition… only here,of course, the dogs had to be dressed up! There was a Labrador dressed as a Scarecrow, a bull terrier in a wedding dress and scarily of all the owners had dressed up to match their dogs. Mmm

Speaking of which, we have our 'mediation' meeting on Wednesday, watch this space…

Our birthday present to the boys was an hour and a half soccer lesson with a professional player called John JoJeff. He is an Aussie guy who used to play with Graeme Souness and Patrick Johnson. He has a reputation here for being really hard on kids; he recently got really cross with a team of kids and made them run laps around a pitch in 90 degrees heat for an hour. I have to say he was brilliant with the boys and pushed them really hard but taught them many new skills. It ended up being almost two hours and Sam said afterwards that it was so exciting!

We are entering the last two weeks of school here. It ends on June 15th so the homework is slowing down but the parties are starting up! Abbie still has a Bar / Bat Mitzvah most Saturdays. It was strange to fill in the forms saying we won't need places for them next year. Although if we were to stay I should have moved the kids away from that awful Principal anyway.

Overall we have been very pleased with the education the kids have had since being here, they are certainly pushed very hard and get a lot of homework and the discipline is much more enforced but often in a very petty way. It is just some of what they teach that is definitely propaganda! You know how the Americans are considered to be arrogant? Well, since living here I can really understand why and how. Bearing in mind that a supposed 80% of them do not have a passport and many do not ever move from the State in which they are born. With this in mind, and remembering just how huge the United States is you begin to see what is happening.

The middle Americans, those in between the East and West coast, are very Church orientated. Mainly, because it is so vast that being part of a church is your social life and forms many communities. These people are, quite literally, told all sorts of false stories and never go or meet anyone else who can tell them otherwise. In many ways they are like third world illiterates but are part of the richest and most powerful country in the world. And THAT is what is so scary. Now we have seen odd bits and pieces of this here in California which is considered to be the most progressive state in the country. Never has it been more brought home to us than this week. One of Abbies' friends was here and stayed for dinner. We all got talking about WW II. This girl is a lovely good Jewish girl and had recently done a school oral presentation on the Holocaust, for which she received an A and, apparently reduced her teacher to tears…. Now, I don't know if many of you are aware but Nigel is quite the WWII expert and is very well read in that arena and so was utterly horrified to listen to this girls interpretation of the Americans role in that war. What she told us had been taught to her, in school, was that it was America that went to war with Germany and defeated them, and that Britain joined the war efforts briefly, in the last two years, to support America!

Can you imagine what is going to be taught in schools here regarding the current war in Iraq?

It reminded Nigel and I of watching the Olympics here when we first arrived and how on TV we only ever saw the sports that Americans were likely to get a medal for. I mean, did you know that playing beach volley ball in tiny, tiny bikinis was an Olympic Sport?

Only the Septics Eh?

June 17th, 2007

THE END OF ONE CHAPTER AND THE BEGINNING OF ANOTHER.

Well, we are down to our final ten days after a mad few weeks of school came to an end. There have been lots of parties, lots of tears and lots of panicking!

Last week we had our leaving party which was organized by Jenn and her hubby Ed.

It was held in Creekside Park, which is behind the school and where they host the Easter Egg Hunt. A perfect setting with Mount Tam and the creek close by. Everyone brought a bottle and Jenn had organized a Taco van to provide the food. Tacos are a Mexican type of food and the guys set it all up and cooked it all fresh in front of us. We each had a huge metal platter, put our chosen filling on top of enormous round Tortilla bread and then gave it all back to him to fold it and put it quickly on the hot plate to seal it. It was yummy!

There was a camera man interviewing all our friends and then us separately. So, we now have two leaving party videos either side of the Atlantic! I dread to think what they said about me! It was a lovely somewhat emotional night, especially for Jenn and I who have become such close friends since we have been here. She is off on her own adventure next week. She and her family are off to live in Barcelona for two months. I'm glad I won't see her the day we actually leave; I would be a blubbering wreck.

For Niges' birthday last December I had got him a skydiving trip, so last week we went to watch him do that. It was at a tiny air base, an hour north of here in wine country at a place called Cloverdale. The guy who ran it was a German bloke who was hysterical, he jumped out of planes wearing what looked like a clowns outfit and flip flops with elastic bands to keep them on his feet! His safety talk was so funny but his language was so shocking he even made me blush! Nige went off in a tiny plane that sounded like a hairdryer. There were no seats and just a flap of curtain for a door! A camera man jumped with him and on the video you can hear the mad German shout

"Long Live the Queen", as he shoved Nigel out of the plane!

Nigel was so breathless when he landed; he said it was the most breathtakingly exhilarating thing he has ever experienced. I almost peed myself laughing in the edit room for the video. There is a wall of shame which is full of pictures of those who have passed out or puked whilst jumping! I laughed so much that the guy showed me some video clips of people who did both. I tell you, you do not want to jump solo the first time!

Friday the 15th was the last day of school so it was gradation day for the 8th graders. That night I was a chaperone for their school dance. In true Californian style it was a real party night. The school hall was beautifully decked out in Chinese red lanterns, there was a red carpet with photographers and as soon as they took the pictures the images were beamed onto a wall inside the hall. Once inside there was a huge bouncy castle, a magician, a graffiti wall where the kids could write messages to friends and teachers, a popcorn machine and lots of other things. It was really well put together, there was also a wall where parents had written to their children including a photo, if their name was, for example, Angela then there was a picture of Angelina Jolie, if it was Cameron then there was a picture of Cameron Diaz etc. I found this a bit weird; they had all written really intense messages about 'keeping the dream alive' and how their darling could be the next Einstein. Personally I found it a bit over the top; after all they were just finishing middle school not scaling Everest! *

To-day was also Abbies 13th birthday. I have decided I am way too young to have a teenager so, from now on I am twenty nine and when anyone asks how old my children are I shall just say four years old, therefore implying I am very young and Leo is my oldest child and that my ovaries are in fact capable of creating more babies! Abbie, Sam and Ben will become my niece and nephews of my older (much older...) sister. Sorted!

To celebrate madams birthday we had a swim and spa day at home. I made up some Pumpkin and Papaya face masks that I found a recipe for online and I did everyones nails and gave them

---

* The video clip of our leaving party can be seen on www.youtube.com. Type in Farewell to the Barretts in the search box

foot massages. The boys did a BBQ with homemade organic burgers and chicken kebabs and we had a henna tattoo artist paint the girls. It was all cucumber water and water melons and the chant for the day was peace and love. The pool was 90 degrees, the sunshine 85 degrees and it was lovely. All her pals had made cards and a photo album for her. They had also put together a tribute CD of all of her years with them at school. I had to leave the room as it made me cry thinking that she will probably never see these friends again.

So, now the parties are over it is time to start packing as of tomorrow. We have been clearing out some of the crap we have accumulated over the last few years.

Who needs colonic irrigation? Give me a bin bag and directions for the tip and it has the same effect for me!

It was really quite surreal this week ordering rental furniture for a house I have never seen, and have no idea if it will even fit through the front door! Something that would have stressed me out a few years ago but now I just think fuck it, what does it matter?

Next Friday a friend is taking us out on his yacht around the Bay to say a last farewell. It all sounds wonderfully romantic but the truth is Abbie and I are likely to barf!

We have now accepted school places for the kids in Maidenhead in Berkshire.

Even little Leo will soon be ready to start big school. This means I shall be job hunting as of next April!

Where did that time go?

He is such a ray of sunshine to us, we laugh everyday at his antics. He loves to sing and dance to an audience using anything at all for a microphone. He uses all my northern terminology but with an American accent!

So, Nige and the boys are off playing soccer, or as I will have to convert back to saying footie and I need to sign off.

Oh yes, our mediation meeting!

Well, we arrived at the appointed offices and sat at the table with two mediators and the dogs owners. Apparently, get this, the Boxer has been on TWO aggressive dog training courses and failed both. It is now exercised on a treadmill that they keep in the garage and only goes out of the house for a walk once a week! They sat there with their beautiful baby in a pram and all I could think was

"Why would you have a dog like that around your baby?'"

One of the mediators really annoyed me by making light of the situation and joking that his Uncle had a Rottweiler dog that he kissed on the face and that people should not fear big breeds of dog. I had to remind him that these dogs had attacked with no warning and *were* considered dangerous! The end result was that when they take the boxer outside then the owner has to wear a harness that the dog is attached to.

Who will police that I wonder?

They did have to sign a document agreeing to this which I have copied and given to our neighbours so that they may inform the authorities if they break this agreement.

I am glad that soon it will no longer be my problem to worry about.

I have enjoyed writing these newsletters, they have been a way for me to channel any frustrations as well as maintaining my promise to 'keep in touch' with multiple people at a time. I have intended for them to be a way of recording our experiences for the kids as I am sure they will forget so much, especially Leo.

I hope you have enjoyed them too and that I have given you an insight of how it is to live here. It has been an incredible journey for us all. As a family we have done so much together and made some fantastic memories to last our lifetime. However, there have been, without a doubt, more negative experiences within a very short space of time then we have ever experienced individually or collectively before.

Sadly and ultimately it has been these that have led to our decision to return home.

Certainly for me it was the devastating experience with the boys last December that put the 'kybosh' on life here for me.

We have learned a lot about the family that caused us all the heartache and how their behaviour seems to have been a pattern at all the schools the child has attended. The worst part in many ways was the lack of any kind of fair treatment we got within the school district. For sure the boys have learned a very hard lesson, and that

is that not all adults tell the truth or can be trusted. But, we do not want to dwell on that nor do we want to detract from all the wonderful and positive experiences we have had.
So, what will we miss?

The fab weather for six months of the year
The great friends we have made
The social life – endless parties!
Eating out cheaply
Spending so much time together

The things we won't miss

The rainy season
Botox bunnies
Rude people
Sir Francis Drake Blvd
School administration
Petty rules and regulation
Helicopter parents

ok, I think I should stop there!

Things I am looking forward to

Decent clothes shopping!
Being nearer to extended family
Not being in the car so much
Four seasons
British humour
Seeing old buildings
A sense of belonging

And of course it goes without saying that wherever we live the door is always open and there's always a bottle of Rioja to share!

BYE!!

EIGHTEEN MONTHS LATER...

Adjusting to life back in England has taken longer than I had anticipated. Now that we have finally bought our own home I think that has helped the children feel more settled.

We opted to move to an area we have never been to before and, so far, things are working out nicely.

The house is a beautiful three storey Edwardian property with an enormous garden and a lawn that is now a football pitch!

All the children can walk to school and to all the local amenities which means I am no longer in the car for several hours a day! Abbie attends an all girl school and is studying for her G.C.S.E's and has joined the local army cadet core which she is very enthusiastic about. I asked her recently what she misses most about Marin and she said the smell?!

It has probably been much harder for her to adapt to life back in England, at 13 years it is difficult to start a new school and have to make new friends, but she is doing well.

Starting a new school was much easier for Sam and Ben as they started senior school along with all the other local children their age. They remain football mad and play both for school and the local town. They do comment on how much faster and harder the games are here!

They remain in contact with their close friends in Marin; the wonders of the Internet mean keeping in touch is fairly easy. When asked what they miss most they say chicken teriyaki burritos!

As for little Leo, he is now at 'big' school full time and loves it. He still talks about some of his friends in Marin but is starting to forget names and places. Recently I showed him some photographs of Hillbilly house but he could not remember living there.

Nigel is probably the one who misses Marin the most! Everytime it rains here he will moan and say,

"I bet it isn't raining in Marin".

I think he has selective memory!

I know he misses catching the ferry to work; the London underground just does not compete really!

Lastly, I am very happy to be home. I completed my Return to Nursing course and am now working as a nurse in the community. Last year I started a bookclub that meets once a month in a local pub and keeps growing in popularity. I have quickly made a nice group of friends and enjoy a great social life. Obviously it is really good to get in the car and be able to drive a relatively short distance to see family too.

I do miss some close friends; last December was so special because Jenn and her son Luke flew out here to celebrate my 40th birthday with me which is a testament to what a special friend she is.

On reflection, our whole experience of living in Marin was a fabulous time for us, as a family. We shared so many good times and adventures together that I think we are all quite open to the idea of living abroad again in the future.

As for going back to Marin?

Of course! We hope to go back in the New Year for a visit, if they will let me back in!

Author Bio

Fiona Barrett was born in Merseyside in 1967. Now she lives in Berkshire, England with her husband and four children. Fiona works as both a Nurse and a Reflexologist in her local community.

Living with the bunnies, a British Familys' exile to Marin County is her first book.